About the author

Tony Buzan, inventor of the now world-famous Mind Maps®, has achieved an astonishing series of accomplishments.

- The world's leading author on the brain and learning with over 80 authored and co-authored books to date and with sales totalling three million and accelerating!
- The world's top lecturer on the brain and learning. The 'Mind Magician', as Tony Buzan has increasingly become known, has lectured to audiences ranging from five-year-old children through disadvantaged students to first-class Oxbridge graduates, to the world's top business directors, and to the leading organisations and governments.
- Founder of the World Memory Championships.
- Founder of the World Speed Reading Championships.
- Black belt in the martial arts.
- Buzan's books and other products have achieved massive success in more than 100 countries and 30 languages, generating revenues in excess of £100 million.
- Inventor of Mind Maps®, the thinking tool described as 'the Swiss army knife of the brain', now used by over 250 million people worldwide.
- Editor, the international journal of MENSA (the high IQ society) from 1968–1971.
- International business consultant to major multinationals including: BP, Barclays International, General Motors, Walt Disney, Oracle, Microsoft, HSBC, British Telecom, IBM, British Airways, etc.
- Consultant and adviser to governments and government organisations including: England, Singapore, Mexico, Australia, the Gulf States and Liechtenstein.
- Olympic Coach.
- Originator of the concepts of Radiant Thinking and Mental Literacy.
- Prize-winning poet.
- Prize-winning athlete.
- A global media personality, having appeared on over 100 hours of national and global television, and over 1000 hours of national and international radio. He has been seen and heard by an estimated three billion-plus people!

Also by Tony Buzan

Books

The Mind Set
  Use Your Head
  Use Your Memory
  The Speed Reading Book
  The Mind Map Book
Get Ahead
Brain S£ll
Super Sell
BrainSmart Leader
Sales Genius
Mind Maps in Medicine
Brain Training
Buzan's Book of Mental World Records
Synapsia (Individual)
Synapsia (89–99 complete set)
The Younger Tongue
Brain Power for Kids
Teach Yourself Revision Guides
(GCSE level in 17 subjects)
Teach Yourself Revision Guides
(A level in 8 subjects)
Teach Yourself Literature Guides
(22 titles)
How to Mind Map
The Power of Spritual Intelligence
The Power of Social Intelligence
The Power of Verbal Intelligence
Head Strong
The Power of Creative Intelligence
Head First
Mind Maps for Kids

Video tapes

Learning with Lana
Developing Family Genius
Get Ahead
If at First . . .
Mindpower

Audio tapes

Use Your Head
Buzan On . . .
  The Brain
  Memory
  Thinking & Creativity
  Success
  Reading
  Mind & Body
  Mind Mapping
Mind Mapping Natural Genius
The Genius Formula
Brain S£ll

Other products

Brain Club – Home Study Plan
Body & Soul Poster (Limited Edition)
Desiderata Reconsidered
Universal Personal Organiser
Mind Map Kit

Software

Mind Manager (CD-ROM)
Mind Manager (Trial CD-ROM)
Mastering Memory
(Computer Software & Manual)

Master Your Memory

Tony Buzan

Dedicated to my dear friends in the Brain Clubs and Buzan Centres

External Editor-in-chief: Vanda North
Special Consultants: Dr Susan Whiting, GMM
Grandmaster Raymond Keene, OBE

Published by BBC Worldwide Limited,
Woodlands, 80 Wood Lane, London W12 0TT

First published in 1988
Revised and updated 1989, 1998
This revised edition published in 2003

ISBN 0 563 48700 3

Mind Map® is a registered trademark of the Buzan Organisation 1990
Mental Literacy® is a registered trademark of the Buzan Organisation 1994
Radiant Thinking® is a registered trademark of the Buzan Organisation 1994

Series design by Ben Cracknell Studios
Illustrations by Alan Burton and Ben Cracknell Studios

Commissioning Editor: Emma Shackleton
Project Editor: Cath Harries

Set in Meridien
Printed and bound in Great Britain by The Bath Press, Bath
Cover printed by Belmont Press Ltd, Northampton

Contents

Appreciation

My heart- and mind-felt thanks to the following for their masterful and memorable performances: to Dr Susan Whiting, Grandmaster of Memory and four-times Women's World Memory Champion, for her creative and unceasing efforts in helping me to refine SEM^3, in helping others understand, appreciate and use it, and for being the current reigning 'SEM^3 Champion'!; to Vanda North, my External Editor-in-Chief, for her dedication and support of the concept and for her utter and joyful dedication to the vision of a Mentally Literate Planet; to International Chess and Mind Sports Grandmaster Raymond Keene, OBE, for his ground-breaking work on the identification and ranking of genius, and for his cogent insights into the body of Shakespeare's works; to Memory Grandmaster Ian Docherty for his on-going help with the development of SEM^3 and for his Master Mind Map, which inspired the Mind Maps you will find in this book; to the wonderful artists Lorraine Gill and Christopher Hedley-Dent for their help in educating me in the appreciation of art and their intensive research support for 'the Artists' section of this book; to my Personal Assistant Lesley Bias who kept all other systems running immaculately while also overseeing the production of this manuscript; to my dear mother, Jean Buzan, whose 'eagle editorial eye' caught over twenty-five errors in the 'finished manuscript'; to my Research Assistant and computer-whiz Susanne Pumpin who gathered much invaluable information and who transferred the bulk of the information in this book from my brain to her computer's brain!; to Dominic O'Brien, six-time and dawn of millennium reigning World Memory Champion, for manifesting everything that this book says is possible; and to my dear original Editor Sheila Ableman, who nurtured all my BBC books to such successful birth and fruition; and to my *new* and cherished Editor, Joanne Osborn, who has worked with me on many other successful publishing projects; to our superb artist and Mind Mapper, Alan Burton, the mnemonic memorability of whose artwork was matched only by the memorability of the witty and creative conversations about the artwork; and to my delightful BBC Editorial team, with a special thanks to Sally Potter and Kelly Davis.

Foreword

by Dominic O'Brien, GMM

(FIRST AND 8 TIMES WORLD MEMORY CHAMPION)

If I told you a story about a schoolboy who failed a number of his 'O' levels, left school aged sixteen, was told by his teachers that he would never amount to anything, but who eventually became the World Memory Champion, you would probably think I was a writer of fiction and that the story could not possibly be true. However, it *is* true. That 'failure of a lad' was me!

After leaving school, travelling and working at various jobs, I saw one day on television a man called Creighton Carvello memorise a pack of cards in just under three minutes. To me this was miraculous, although it was obviously not a trick. Creighton really had memorised the cards in that staggeringly short time.

I thought: 'I have a brain the same as he has. If he can do that marvellous feat, there must be a method by which I can also do it.' I set about training myself.

After a few months, I reached the 'Holy Grail' of three minutes. Wondering what to do next with my rapidly growing 'memory muscle', I heard of the first World Memory Championships in 1991, organised by the author of the book you are now reading, Tony Buzan. I entered the competition and after some mighty mental combat was declared the first World Memory Champion.

The foundation principles I used to achieve my World Championships are those you will find outlined in Tony Buzan's book. If you apply these principles to the matrices of knowledge that *Master Your Memory* so vividly portrays, you will be able to bestride both the world of memory and the world of knowledge simultaneously, giving yourself the advantages that I found such training and application gave to me: greater self-confidence, a growing mastery of my imagination, improved creativity, vastly improved perceptual skills, and, yes, a much higher IQ!

I feel honoured to be able to recommend this enlightening book, whose author has so many credentials. Besides holding the World Record for Creative IQ, Tony is the author of over twenty best sellers about the brain and learning. He has established the Brain Foundation, is co-founder of the Mind Sports Olympiad and creator of the now world-famous Mind Maps. He was named by Forbes Magazine as one of five top international lecturers, along with Mikhail Gorbachev, Henry Kissinger and Margaret Thatcher. To my mind, Tony is one of the world's most effective communicators, both verbally and in the written word.

Congratulations on starting a journey I know will change your life magnificently.

Dominic O'Brien

Foreword

by Dr Susan Whiting, GMM

(FIRST CONTESTED AND REIGNING WOMEN'S WORLD MEMORY CHAMPION)

All those who are seriously interested in improving their memories and that should mean everyone because we all have memories that can be improved – should study *Master Your Memory*.

I first came across this book some years ago, after I had given up a challenging professional career to look after my young family. Like many people in similar situations, I found myself needing some additional mental stimulation. Also, I suppose I had always been curious about memory techniques, especially when it came to learning more easily for exams and generally remembering all those things that life demands.

Fortunately, I was introduced to some of Tony Buzan's work and read a first edition of *Master Your Memory*. The book took me completely by surprise – I had no idea memorising information could be fun! After all, revising for exams was always tedious and, dare I say it, boring. Suddenly memorising became not only possible but pleasurable, and expanding my memory developed into a hobby.

Using the memory techniques that I found in Tony's work led on to other things, but it was certainly not a case of memorising for the sake of it. Having memorised many of the composers, I now understand and can relate better to the period in which they composed. My mind is somehow more focused and I appreciate their music even more. Because I now have a 'hook' for each of them in my brain, I can easily add further information.

Art and artists had never been part of my previous studies, but settling down and learning about them paid real dividends. For a start, it was enjoyable to learn something completely new to me, and when I visited the National Gallery you can imagine my delight when in room after room I discovered paintings I had memorised. I could tell my children all sorts of details about the artist and particular styles – a very satisfying experience, and not just because the children looked on Mummy with a new respect.

All of this culminated in my becoming the Women's World Memory Champion in 1994 and the first-ever female Grand Master of Memory in 1996.

How I wish that I had discovered these memory techniques earlier in life, before I had to take all my exams! You, the reader, have precisely that opportunity. This book will teach you how to learn in the most enjoyable way – but be warned, it can become quite addictive!

Susan Whiting

Note on Recommended SEM³ locations

The Mnemons, a group found by the author and led by Dr Sue Whiting GM, recommend and are using the following SEM3 locations for some of the major areas of knowledge:

Polymathic Area	SEM^3 Section
Geniuses	1000–1199
Artists	1200–1399
Composers	1400–1599
Scientists	1600–1799
Writers	1800–1999
Monarchs	2000–2099
Geography	4000–4099
Languages	5000–5999
Shakespeare	7000–7499
The Elements	8000–8199
The Human Body	8200–8599
Your Life	9000–10,000+!

A Story You Will Remember for the Rest of Your Life

A student sat, frightened and enthralled. It was the first lesson of his first day at university. He, like the others in his class, had been forewarned that Professor Clark was not only the most brilliant graduate in English the university had ever had; he also looked down on his students from the height of his genius, and used his mental might to embarrass and confuse them. The Professor had deliberately come in late – to add to the tension!

Professor Clark strode nonchalantly into the room, and scanned the class with fiery eyes and a derisive smile.

Rather than going to his desk and ordering his papers in preparation, he stopped in *front* of his desk, clasped his hands firmly behind his back, and, with that same intent stare accompanied by a sneer, he said, *'First year English? I'll call the roll.'* He then began to bark out, machine-gun fashion, the names of the petrified students:

'Abrahamson?'	'Here, sir!'
'Adams?'	'Here, sir!'
'Barlow?'	'Here, sir!'
'Bush?'	'Here, sir!'
'Buzan?'	'Here, sir!' . . .

When he came to the next name he barked out 'Cartland', to which there was a deathly silence. Looking even more intently, the Professor, like some Grand Inquisitor, made soul-burning eye contact with each petrified student, as if expecting them to 'own up' to their already-identified name. Still receiving no response, he sighed deeply, and said, at twice the speed of normal speech: 'Cartland?... Jeremy Cartland, address 2761 West Third Avenue; phone number 794 6231; date of birth September 25th 1941;

mother's name Jean, father's name Gordon;... *Cartland!?'* Still no response! The silence became almost unbearable until, at exactly the right moment, he punctuated it with a shouted and terminal **'Absent!'**

And so on and on the Professor continued, calling the roll without hesitation. Whenever a student was absent he would go through the same 'Cartland Routine', presenting the entire database about the absentee even though he could have had no way of knowing, on this first day, who was going to be present and who was going to be absent, even though he had never seen any one of the students before. To everyone in the class it became increasingly apparent that he knew, in the same astounding detail, the same basic biographical information about each of them.

When he had completed the roll call with 'Zygotski?' ... 'Here, Sir!', he looked at the students sardonically and said, with a droll smile, 'That means Cartland, Chapman, Harkstone, Hughes, Luxmore, Mears and Tovey are absent!' He paused again, and then said: 'I'll make a note of that ... *some time!'*

So saying, he turned and left the room in stunned silence.

To the enthralled student it was one of those moments where a life's 'Impossible Dream' became possible: the dream of training his memory so that it could, in a multitude of special situations, function perfectly.

To be able to remember the names and dates of birth and death and all the important facts about the major artists, composers, writers and other 'greats'!

To be able to remember languages!

To be able to remember the giant catalogues of data from biology and chemistry!

To be able to remember any list he wanted!

To be able to remember like the Professor!

He leapt out of his seat, charged out of the classroom and caught up with Professor Clark in the hallway. He blurted out his question: 'Sir, how did you do *that?!'* With the same imperious manner, the Professor responded, 'Because, son, I'm a Genius!' And once again turned away, not hearing the student's mumbled response, 'Yes, sir, I know, but *still,* how did you *do* that?!'

For two months he pestered 'The Genius', who finally befriended him, and surreptitiously in class translated for him 'the magic formula' for constructing the memory system that had allowed him to so dazzle the students on that memorable first day.

For the next 20 years the student devoured every book he could find on memory, creativity and the nature of the human brain, with the vision constantly in mind of creating new Super Memory Systems that went beyond even what his Professor had been able to accomplish.

The first of these was the Memory Mind Map, a 'Swiss army knife thinking tool for the brain', that allowed the user not only to remember with accuracy and flexibility but also to create, plan, think, learn and communicate on the basis of that memory.

After the Mind Map came the giant, enjoyable and easy-to-use Super Matrix Memory System that would act as a database, allowing people to have immediate access to whatever major information structures were important and necessary to them.

After 25 years, the New System emerged. The enthralled student was me! The one to whom I offer this New System, with delight, is you.

Master Your Memory and How to Use It

To start you off on what will be the major intellectual adventure of your life, the first section of this book gives you immediate proof that your own memory can easily and successfully complete a memory task normally only accomplished by one person in a hundred.

When you have proved that your own memory can work at this level, you will be shown how Memory (mnemonic) Systems were originally envisioned by the Ancient Greeks, and how they have been developed to the present day.

Next you will be introduced to the Memory Principles, which will give you the building blocks with which to structure your newly enhanced memory skills. This will be combined with a concomitant development of all your senses.

Following this, you will be introduced to the most up-to-date modern brain research, especially that involving the left and right cerebral cortex and the relationships between the upper, mid- and hind-brain. Here you will find out how the Memory Principles link with our modern knowledge of how your brain works.

Armed with the knowledge of how the Principles work, of how your senses can be enhanced, and of how your brain skills can be used appropriately, you will realise something amazing: that, in the process of successfully completing your first memory task, you not only used the fundamental principles invented by the Greeks, you also innocently applied state-of-the-art information on your brain to its excellent functioning!

From this you will be introduced to the first significant Memory System – the Major System. It is this system that has been used by most of the world's top memory performers, mnemonists and mental athletes such as those who compete in the Memoriad and the World Memory Championships. First you will be shown how to memorise a 10-item shopping list using the Major System, then immediately how to multiply your ability *10 times* in order to remember 100 items.

Taking the steps from 100 to 1000 to *10,000* may seem like an impossible dream. To show you that it is *completely* possible, you will be guided through recent experiments on learning and memory which prove that your brain can remember not only 10,000 items, but even more, with astonishing accuracy.

Further evidence will be drawn from some of the great brains in history (who had brains just like yours!), with examples showing the extraordinary memory feats of which the human brain is capable. I emphasise that their brains were the same as yours; they simply knew how to use them in the manner outlined in *Master Your Memory*.

By this stage you will be capable of absorbing comfortably the Self-Enhancing Master Memory Matrix (SEM^3). Having mastered the Matrix, you will be able to use it to learn and remember any significant database you wish.

You will then be in possession of the basic building blocks of knowledge in music, art, literature, science, astronomy, languages, history and world geography.

You will discover that, in the very act of developing your memory systems and of remembering the basic architectural structure of knowledge, you will be making your 'Memory Muscle' significantly more powerful and you will also be increasing your mental powers of concentration and creativity.

Onword

We begin by proving to you that your memory is far better than you think!

Proof That Your Memory Can Work:

the Simple and Effective Link System

Preview

- The Test
- Memorising the Planets of the Solar System

The memory test you are about to take involves the Planets of the Solar System. Having researched this area for the last 25 years, I have found that, in the average audience of 1000 people, the following statistics apply:

1   Nine hundred people out of 1000 have learnt and at some time memorised the Planets.
2   In each individual's lifetime, they have been 'exposed' to this information, either at school, or through various media, for a total number of hours ranging between 10 and 100.
3   One hundred out of 1000 *think* they know how many Planets there are in the Solar System.
4   Forty out of 1000 know they know how many.
5   Ten *think* they know the order of the Planets from the Sun to the farthest Planet.
6   Ten out of 1000 would be willing to bet on it!

The reason for this staggering loss of knowledge lies in the fact that we are never taught *how* to remember.

Check your knowledge and experience in this particular memory task:

- Did you learn the Planets of the Solar System, and if so, how many times and over what period of time?

- Do you know the currently accepted *number* of Planets in the Solar System?
- Do your know their *names*?
- Do you know the *normal order* of the Planets in the Solar System?

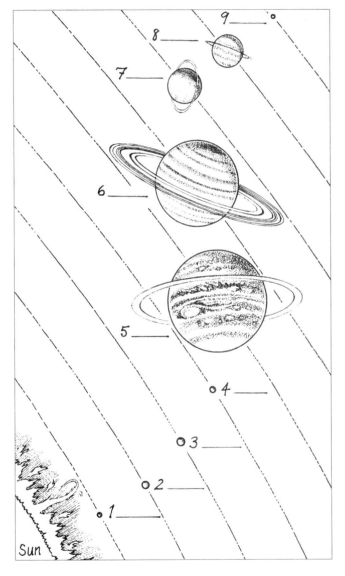

Fig. 1 The nine Planets of our Solar System – one of the most difficult memory tasks confronted by the people on the third one! For how to memorise the Planets for the rest of your life, see page 20

The Test

Write down the names of all the Planets of our Solar System. Now, using the illustration on page 19, with the Sun in the bottom left-hand corner, put the planet names where you think they should go next to the numbers 1–9. (Just to give you a clue – Sagittarius is not a planet!) When completed, see below for the correct planet order. Give yourself one mark for each planet correctly placed. If you have the correct planet name but in the wrong place, you score 0, in the same way as you would if you mixed up the digits of a telephone number! The average score around the world on this test is between one and two, so don't worry if yours is a low score.

Memorising the Planets of the Solar System

The following exercise will change the way you use your memory for ever, increase your memory power, and enable you to complete a memory task that most people never accomplish in a lifetime!

Follow the instructions carefully, let your imagination run free, and prepare to be amazed.

There are *nine* Planets in the Solar System.

In order from the Sun, they are:

1   Mercury (small)
2   Venus (small)
3   Earth (small)
4   Mars (small)
5   Jupiter (big)
6   Saturn (big)
7   Uranus (big)
8   Neptune (big)
9   Pluto (small)

In order to memorise the Planets for *life* you are going to use a Linking System, in conjunction with your imagination, to create a linked and fantastic story. If you follow it carefully and completely, it will be harder for you to forget than to remember!

Imagine that in front of you, where you are currently reading, is a glorious **SUN**. See it clearly, feel its heat, and admire its orange/red glow. Imagine, next to the Sun, a little (it's a little Planet) thermometer, filled with that liquid metal that measures temperature: **MERCURY**.

Imagine that the Sun heats up, and eventually becomes so hot that it bursts the thermometer. You see all over the desk or floor, in front of you, tiny balls of that liquid metal Mercury. Next you imagine that, rushing in to see what happens, and standing by your side, comes the most beautiful little goddess. Colour her, clothe her (optional!), perfume her, design her as you will. What shall we call our little goddess? Yes, **VENUS**!

You focus so intently on Venus with all your senses, that she becomes almost a living physical reality in front of you. You see Venus play like a child with the scattered mercury, and finally manage to pick up one of the mercury globules. She is so delighted that she throws it in a giant arc way up in the sky (which you see, as light glistens off it throughout its journey), until it hurtles down from on high and lands in your garden with a gigantic 'thump'!, which you both hear and feel as a bodily vibration.

And on what planet is your garden? **EARTH**.

Because of the power of her throw, and the height of the arc, when the globule lands it creates a small crater which sprays earth (EARTH) into your neighbour's garden.

In this fantasy you imagine that your neighbour is a little (it's a little Planet), red-faced (it's a red Planet), angry and war-like character carrying a chocolate bar in his leading hand! And who is this God of War? **MARS**.

Mars is furious that the earth has gone into his garden, and is just about to attack you when, striding on to the scene, comes a giant so large and powerful that he shakes the very foundations (and you must *feel them*) of where you are. See him standing a hundred feet tall, and make him as real as you made Venus. He tells Mars to calm down, which Mars immediately does, for this new giant, with a giant cow-lick 'J' on his forehead, is your best friend as well as being the king of the gods, the fifth Planet: **JUPITER**.

As you look up to the hundred-foot-high Jupiter, you see the word 'SUN' emblazoned in flashing gold letters across the giant T-shirt on his enormous chest. Each of these gigantic letters stands for the first letter of each of the next three big Planets of the Solar System: **SATURN, URANUS, NEPTUNE**.

Sitting on Jupiter's head, barking his little heart out with humour because he thinks the episode has been so hilarious, is a little (little because the Planet is so small) Walt Disney dog by the name of **PLUTO**.

Re-run this fantasy in your mind, and then see how difficult it is to forget!

In the continuing studies of people's memorisation of the Planets, it was found that, before memorising them with the Memory Principles:

(a) Eight hundred out of 1000 people didn't really care about the Planets and seldom paid attention to information about them.

(b) One hundred out of 1000 felt interested in the Planets.

(c) One hundred out of 1000 were actively uninterested and/or disliked the Planets.

After memorising the Planets with imagination and the Link System, virtually every one of the 1000 became actively interested.

This on-going study illustrates the very significant fact that if the human brain receives data that is rapidly forgotten or it becomes confused, it will reject further data in that subject area. As time goes on, the more information is presented to the brain in the given area, the more it will block that information and the less it will learn, often eventually blocking the information altogether.

If the brain, on the other hand, has information in an organised and memorable matrix, each new bit of information will automatically link to the existing information, naturally building into the patterns of recognition, understanding and memory that we call knowledge.

For example, if you hear that a space probe has been sent to Venus and you do *not* know where Venus lies within the Solar System, the first thing your brain will be confronted with is confusion. You will not know which way the probe has gone from the Earth, whether Venus is hot or cold, what its relationship is to the Sun and why anyone should send a space probe there in the first place. Consequently, you will react by rejecting the information.

If, on the other hand, you *know* that Venus is the second Planet out from the Sun, and is the one inside Earth's orbit that is nearest to Earth, you will know that, as the space probe goes to Venus, it will be going to a Planet that is nearer to the Sun and therefore hotter than Earth. Your mind will therefore have a mental image of direction, temperature, and nearness to Earth, and will *automatically* make appropriate associations. At the same time as your mind is doing this, it will also be confirming your knowledge of the other Planets. Thus, the more you know, *and remember*, the more easily and automatically you begin to know more.

Thus you quickly come to realise that the more structured knowledge you have in your memory, especially if it is in matrix form, the easier it is to remember more. Your memory is so extraordinary that, once given these basic matrices, it will continue to link new information to them *without your conscious effort*. You might wish to give yourself a head start by learning details of all the Planets (see chapter 19).

Conversely, if you do not have basic memory and knowledge structures, the more your mind confronts knowledge, the more it disconnects from it, leaving you with a growing 'memory of all that you have forgotten and not learnt'!

Thus, if you use your memory well, you can look forward to a life of increasing memory skills, expanding knowledge, accelerating ease of learning and, as a consequence of all these, greater mastery of your memory and therefore greater fun.

You have just completed a 'thought experiment' which used techniques identical to those used by the Great Geniuses throughout history. As soon as you phone or meet a friend or family member, teach them what you have just learnt – it will be an excellent review for you, will 'stamp' the memory more firmly in your brain, and will give them a useful gift. Encourage them to do the same, and within a few years you will have initiated that which will enable everybody on Earth to know where Earth is!

Onword

In the next chapter you will be introduced to the history of memory (mnemonic) systems, and will receive the first of a number of insights into why your brain was able to do so remarkably well in the task you have just successfully completed.

Memory –
the Principles
and Techniques

Preview

- The Background
- The Three Memory Principles
- The 12 Memory Techniques
- Modern Confirmation of the Greeks
- Creativity and Memory
- Memory Systems Are Not 'Tricks'
- Increasingly Advanced Systems

Did you know that over 95 per cent of people who drive a car have accomplished one of the most phenomenal forgetting tasks imaginable?!

They have driven their car to a shopping centre, an airport, a theatre, a friend's, and, having completed their tasks, have returned only to find they have *completely* lost (i.e. forgotten the location of) their car.

How is this *possible*?! It is a vehicle weighing three tonnes, it is theirs, they got into it, they drove it, they aimed it at the parking spot, they parked it, they shut off the engine, they got out of the car, they closed the door, and they locked it.

Surely the brain could not possibly forget such a thing?

As you read this chapter, you will realise that, not only were they capable of forgetting in such a situation, it is actually *predictable* that they would forget, for they did not apply the very essences of which memory is composed. Read on, and you will begin to see why . . .

Now check the Planet Story once more, running through it very carefully, *this* time checking to see how many of the left and right cortical skills are employed in the system. You will find it is virtually all of them!

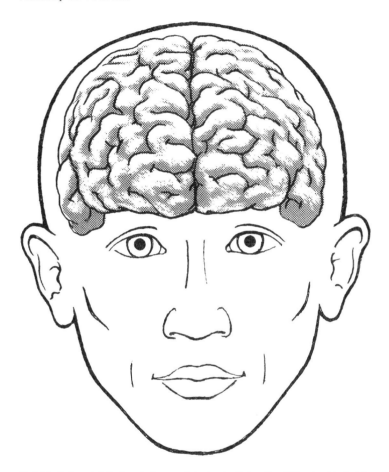

Fig 2 The left and right hemispheres of the brain. Using the skill sets of *both* sides dramatically improves the memory.

Creativity and Memory

From the theory you have understood and the exercise you have already completed on the memorisation of the Planets, the incredibly close link between memory *properly practised* and creativity will be starting to become clear.

The prime engine of your creativity is your IMAGINATION. The creative genius goes on imaginative journeys, taking people into original and previously unexplored realms. There, new ASSOCIATIONS give rise to the new realisations that the world calls the creative breakthroughs – the works of mental genius that can shift the course of history.

So it was with Leonardo da Vinci, Darwin, Archimedes, Newton, Cézanne and Einstein.

Thus it becomes clear that memory is the use of imagination and association to hold the past in its appropriate place and to re-CREATE the past in the present; whereas creativity is the use of imagination and association to plant the present thought in the future, and to re-CREATE the present thought, whether it be a poem, a symphony, a scientific relationship, a building, or a spaceship, in some future time.

The important point here is that, although the name and purposes may be slightly different, the *underlying principles* of IMAGINATION and ASSOCIATION are identical. Therefore, whenever you are practising or applying memory techniques, you are *at the same time* practising and enhancing your powers of creativity.

These exercises are very much to the brain as gymnastic exercises are to the body. The more you exercise in the 'Gymnasium of Mnemonics', the more the 'muscles' of your memory and creativity will be developed.

Carrying this idea a little further, a new formula for developing your genius emerges: the more Energy you put into developing your Memory, the more your Creativity will grow. You have an infinite capacity to do this. In other words energy plus and 'into' memory equals infinite creativity. The formula can be written:

$$E \rightarrow M = C^{\infty}$$

The New Mental formula that demonstrates that if you put energy into your memory you will not only produce a perfect memory, but an expanding and potentially infinite creativity.

The SEM^3 Memory System allows you to embark on the journey towards both infinite memory and creativity.

Memory Systems Are Not 'Tricks'

Because they are so incredibly effective, and because in recent centuries we have tended to denigrate the brain's abilities, many people think that memory systems must in some way be 'unreal' or 'not natural' and therefore some form of trick. However, our new knowledge of the function of the brain and memory has shown us that the reverse is true: that our 'normal' way of using our memories is unnatural and counter-productive, and that the initial realisations of early civilisations, such as the Greeks, were indeed the appropriate and *natural* first steps towards unlocking the limitless powers and vaults of our memories.

Brain Bites

In the last eight World Memory Championships, all the Grandmasters of Memory (and especially the World Memory Champions Dominic O'Brien and Dr Susan Whiting) have confirmed that the more they have practised with mnemonics, the more their natural and normal memories have expanded.

Increasingly Advanced Systems

From the basic Link System, the early practitioners of memory realised that far more advanced and sophisticated systems could be developed (for further Special Systems, see *Use Your Memory* by the author, BBC Worldwide), and that the memorisation of much more complicated data could be made as easy as the memorisation of the Planets.

Onword

One of the most successful of all such systems was the Major System, which is outlined in the next chapter. The Major System is the first giant step in mastering SEM^3.

The Major System 5

**Preview**
- Memorising the Major System Code
- Memorising Dates, Phone, Card and Code Numbers
- The Major System 'One Hundred'
- Making the Major System Your Own
- From 100 to 10,000 in One Easy Bound!

The secret code you are about to learn is the one that Professor Clark

surreptitiously put on the board on that magical day some 38 years ago

(see page 14).

You can now begin to see how Professor Clark performed his extraordinary memory feat in front of those entranced first-year university students. In order to remember all that specific information, he had to apply the Memory Principle of order and sequence. How did he do that? The Major System!

The Major System was devised in the mid-seventeenth century by Stanislaus Mink von Wennsshein. Von Wennsshein's objective was to create a memory system that would convert numbers into letters and letters into numbers, thus allowing the memoriser to make words out of any combination of numbers, and numbers out of any combination of letters.

In the eighteenth century the system was modified and improved by an Englishman, Dr Richard Grey.

In converting numbers to letters, the Major System has a special code, devised so that, by its very nature, it allows itself to be memorised. The code is as follows:

Using the Major System, and applying the Memory Principles and Techniques exactly as you did when memorising the Planets, you might memorise the shopping list in the following way:

1   **1 – Day/Bananas**: Instead of the dawn rising (a good image for day), imagine a giant banana oozing up above the horizon, suffusing the sky with a yellow light. As you did with number 1, see, smell, taste and touch the banana.

2   **2 – Noah/Apples**: In this example you might imagine Noah standing at the front of his ark in the middle of the storm, juggling with beautiful bright red and green apples, taking scrumptious bites out of them as he juggles, and throwing them one by one to all the animals on the ark, they too delighting in the feast!

3   **3 – Ma/Shoe polish**: Imagine your Ma or a friend's Ma polishing a pair of beautiful leather shoes. See the scene extremely clearly. Smell both the leather and the polish. Hear the moving brush across the leather. And then to add humour, imagine that your mother decides to polish her own face!

The more you invent your own exaggerated images the better, for personal association is virtually always more memorable than that suggested or given by someone else. With the remaining seven items, therefore, apply the Memory Principles to the shopping list, making sure that whenever you are in doubt, you add more imagination and more sensuality. Once you have applied the Memory Principles to the memorisation of the list, test yourself, or get someone else to test you. Should you miss an item, go back to it, analyse where the weakness was, and strengthen your association.

By the time you have finished the full 10, you will have advanced from the basic Link System that you used for memorising the Planets, to the first Great Peg System. Peg Systems, like the Major System, use special, permanent and standard lists of Key Memory Images, on which you can attach whatever you wish to memorise, as you have just done with the first 10.

To prove just how good you are, and without looking at either the Major System itself on page 35 or the shopping list on page 36, jot down the first 10 words of the Major System, and the shopping items you memorised with them.

Making the Major System Your Own

For the next two to three days, play with the Major System, refining your Key Memory Images, accelerating your speed, and making sure that in the memorisation of it you use the Memory Principles and Techniques and all your cortical skills. This system should become as natural to you as your name, address and phone number. For advanced particular applications of this system, see *Use Your Memory*. The rest of *Master Your Memory* uses the Major System to help you leap from 100 to 10,000 Key Memory Images, and also to give you the ultimate 'Memory Gymnasium'.

From 100 to 10,000 in One Easy Bound!

Having established the Basic One Hundred, it is now possible, using a system which helps memorise itself, to develop the 10,000 memory system: The Self-Enhancing Master Memory Matrix (SEM^3).

SEM^3 will enable you to memorise not only all the information contained in *Master Your Memory*, but *any* list that may be of importance to you. For those of you using the Universal Personal Organiser (UPO) diary system (available from the Buzan Centre, see page 192), SEM^3 will also enable you to memorise, should you wish, not only the major events of each year of your life but *every day* of your life!

Onword

The following chapter proves that you can do it, explains the Self-Enhancing Master Memory Matrix in detail, and shows you how to use and apply it.

The Self-Enhancing Master Memory Matrix (SEM³): the Total Learning Memory Technique

Before developing a system for the memorisation of 10,000 items,

it is important to find out whether the brain can easily handle such

a matrix. Both research and history indicate that the human brain

can handle it with ease.

The Experimental Evidence

In 1970, Ralph N. Haber reported the following experiment in *Scientific American:* subjects were shown a series of 2560 photographic slides at a rate of one every ten seconds. The total of seven hours of viewing was split into several separate sessions over a period of days, and, one hour after the last slide had been shown on the last day, the subjects were tested for recognition. They were shown 280 pairs of slides in which one member of each pair was a picture from the series they had seen, while the other was from a similar set which they had not seen. On average their recognition, even after such a drawn-out showing, was between 85 to 95 per cent accurate.

A second experiment was performed in which the presentation rate was speeded up ten times, to one image every second, and the results were identical.

A third experiment, in which the new high rate of presentation was maintained, but the pictures were shown as a mirror image, still produced identically high results.

Haber commented: 'these experiments with pictorial stimulae suggest that *recognition of pictures is essentially perfect*. The results would probably have been the same if we had used 25,000 pictures instead of 2500.'

In a further experiment reported by R. S. Nickerson in the *Canadian Journal of Psychology*, subjects were presented, at the rate of one per second, with 600 pictures, and tested immediately after the presentation. Recognition accuracy was 98 per cent.

Nickerson expanded on this research, subsequently presenting subjects with 10,000 pictures, making sure that the pictures were vivid (i.e. applied the Mnemonic Principles). With the vivid pictures, subjects were recalling 9996 out of 10,000 correctly!! When these results were extrapolated, it was estimated by the experimenters that if the subjects had been shown a million pictures rather than 10,000, they would have recognised 986,300.

The conclusion was: 'the capacity of recognition memory for pictures is almost limitless, when measured under appropriate conditions', according to Lionel Standing in his article 'Learning 10,000 Pictures' in the *Quarterly Journal of Experimental Psychology*.

With this evidence, it becomes apparent that the Self-Enhancing Master Memory Matrix, if used in conjunction with the Memory Principles, can be easily handled by your brain. Further evidence from the great memorisers confirms this.

The Great Memorisers

The great memorisers had brains which were the same as everyone else's. They simply used them more effectively. Pick your own favourites from those that follow, and make them your role models. This will be the first step in building up your internal intellectual master-mind group of teachers and guides.

1   **Antonio di Marco Magliabechi** was able to read entire books, and memorise them without missing a single word or punctuation mark. He eventually memorised the entire library of the Grand Duke of Tuscany.

2   **Professor A.C. Aitken**, Professor of Mathematics at the University of Edinburgh, was easily able to remember the first 1000 decimal places of the value of Pi – forwards and backwards.

The Self-Enhancing Master Memory Matrix (SEM³)

The Self-Enhancing Master Memory Matrix allows you, by using the same Memory Principles, to expand from 100 to 10,000 as quickly as you can visualise.

Using the Basic One Hundred from the Major System, you multiply this system by 10, giving you a system of 1000; you then multiply the 1000 system by 10, giving you a system of 10,000.

To create the list of 1000 (0–999), you use the Basic One Hundred, repeated in different aspects of your visual senses.

To create the system of 10,000, you once again use the Basic One Hundred in multiple ways, incorporating each of your senses of vision, sound, smell, taste, touch and sensation, as well as basic data from the physical kingdoms.

By creating a system using such elements, you are at the same time using all of those aspects of your brain that feed your memory skills. You are creating a giant mental gymnasium, which will allow you not only to memorise any list you wish, but which will at the same time provide you with on-going mental work-outs that increase every aspect of your 'Mental Muscle' while simultaneously giving you the opportunity to play infinite games. You construct your Self-Enhancing Master Memory Matrix in the following manner:

100–999	Vision
1000–1999	Sound
2000–2999	Smell
3000–3999	Taste
4000–4999	Touch
5000–5999	Sensation
6000–6999	Animals
7000–7999	Birds
8000–8999	The Rainbow
9000–9999	The Solar System

For the numbers 100 to 999 you use **VISION**; in other words, you focus on you *seeing* the image you wish to remember as your Key Memory Image. For 1000 to 1999, you use **SOUND**, focusing on your *hearing* for each image. For 2000 to 2999, you use your sense of **SMELL**, focusing on your memory images of this sense. And so on, for each thousand, using, sequentially, **TASTE, TOUCH, SENSATION, ANIMALS, BIRDS, THE COLOURS OF THE RAINBOW** and **THE SOLAR SYSTEM**.

For each separate 100 of each 1000, you have a specific Vision, a specific Sound, a specific Smell, etc. Thus, referring to the Matrix on page 42, your specific visions for the separate 100s from 100 to 999 are Dinosaur, Nobility, Moonlight, Ravine, Lightning, Church, Concorde, Fire and Painting.

For example, keeping 0–99 as your Basic 100 Matrix, and using nine Vision-images to get you from 100 to 999, you would do the following:

101 might simply be a giant dinosaur with its head rising above the horizon next to the sun at the beginning of a new *day;* 140 would be your same dinosaur leading an incredibly noisy, thundering and exciting dinosaur *race.* Whatever you wish to memorise as your 101st or 140th items would be attached to these SEM^3 images using the Basic Memory Principles.

Moving up in the first 1000, all still related to the first of your synaesthesia elements, Vision, all items from 700 to 799 would still be the basic code items, but in this instance connected to the image of Concorde. Thus 706 might be Concorde with its bent nose as a giant jaw; 795 could be Concorde with a giant ball for its wheels. Again, any item you wish to attach to these images would be attached using the Memory Principles.

Similarly, for 3000 to 3999, each separate hundred in the progression would have a Taste image attached to the basic hundred, in this instance Spaghetti, Tomato, Nuts, Mango, Rhubarb, Lemon, Cherry, Custard, Fudge and Banana.

To enable you to identify and memorise SEM^3 more easily, a matrix of the 100 divisions is on page 42.

To gain access to any number from 0 to 9999, you use the simple mental process outlined in the section entitled How to Use Your Self-Enhancing Master Memory Matrix (page 46).

When creating your images, which you should do as a game, as well as a mental exercise and mental brain training, make sure that in your Key Memory Images for each of the different senses, you emphasise the sense. Thus, for 4143, touch combined with damp combined with ram, but your main memory device here is to *feel* the wetness of its fur, its horns, its muzzle, and the smell of damp fur.

By using this Self-Enhancing Master Memory Matrix, you will not only be developing a system that enables you to memorise 10,000 items with the ease of Haber and Nickerson's experimental subjects, but you will also be training each one of your sensory areas, which will have a profound and positive influence on all other aspects of your life. This will include a positive influence on your health. Inability to remember, and subsequent frustration and annoyance at that inability, is often a major cause of stress and disease. This in itself creates a worsening memory. By using SEM^3, you will be reversing the trend.

In many ways you will be creating a positive spiral in which the more you practise your Memory Techniques, the more your general memory will improve; the more you add your knowledge lists to your memory matrix, the more you will be increasing the probability of automatic learning; and the more you do all this, the more automatically *all* of your various intelligences and mental skills will be improved.

The following chapters outline many of the major memory lists which, like the Planets, are supposed to be learnt for life but which are usually forgotten. Once they are learnt, they form giant foundations from which your brain can, with the ease and facility of 'The Greats', continue on its journey to wisdom.

The Superlist chapters are as follows:

8 Artists
9 Composers
10 Writers
11 Geniuses
12 Shakespeare
13 Vocabulary
14 Languages
15 Countries/Capitals
16 Kings and Queens of England
17 Human Body – Musculature
18 Elements
19 Solar System
20 Memorising Your Life

The suggested approach to the following Superlists, is to select the ones you wish to memorise, organise your Self-Enhancing Master Memory Matrix appropriately, and commence the exercise of remembering them. Throughout, apply the Memory Principles and Techniques.

To assist you with the construction and organisation of your Superlists refer to the Note on page 11 for recommended SEM^3 locations. From this point on, it is useful to develop further

How to Use Your Self- Enhancing Master Memory Matrix

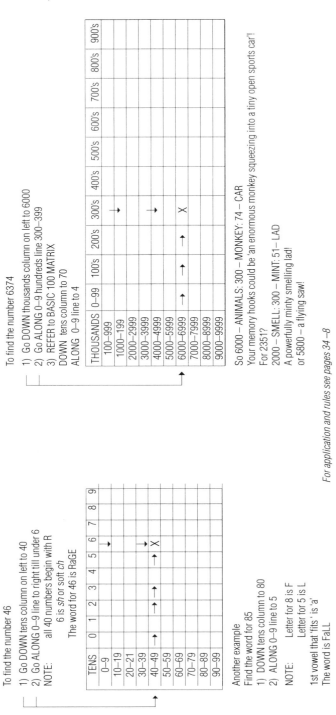

MAJOR SYSTEM – BASIC 100

To find the number 46
1) Go DOWN tens column on left to 40
2) Go ALONG 0–9 line to right till under 6
NOTE: all 40 numbers begin with R
6 is *sh* or soft *ch*
The word for 46 is RaGE

TENS	0	1	2	3	4	5	6	7	8	9
0–9										
10–19										
20–21										
30–39										
40–49						→X				
50–59						↑				
60–69					↑					
70–79				↑						
80–89			↑							
90–99							→			

Another example
Find the word for 85
1) DOWN tens column to 80
2) ALONG 0–9 line to 5
NOTE: Letter for 8 is F
Letter for 5 is L
1st vowel that 'fits' is 'a'
The word is FaLL

SEM 3   100–9999

To find the number 6374
1) Go DOWN thousands column on left to 6000
2) Go ALONG 0–9 hundreds line 300–399
3) REFER to BASIC 100 MATRIX
DOWN tens column to 70
ALONG 0–9 line to 4

THOUSANDS	0–99	100's	200's	300's	400's	500's	600's	700's	800's	900's
100–999										
1000–199				→						
2000–2999										
3000–3999				→						
4000–4999										
5000–5999				X						
6000–6999	↑	↑	↑							
7000–7999										
8000–8999										
9000–9999										

So 6000 – ANIMALS: 300 – MONKEY: 74 – CAR
Your memory hooks could be 'an enormous monkey squeezing into a tiny open sports car'!
For 2351?
2000 – SMELL: 300 – MINT: 51– LAD
A powerfully minty smelling lad!
or 5800 – a flying saw!

For application and rules see pages 34 –8

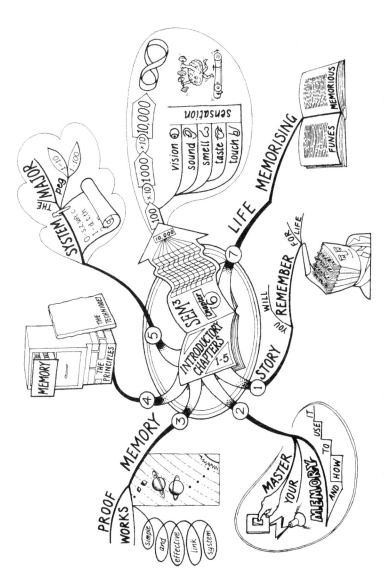

Fig 3 Mind Map of chapters 1–6. When you make your own Mind Maps, you can use colour to make the various branches even more memorable.

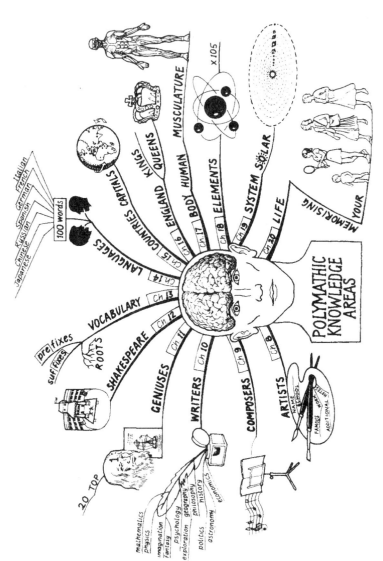

Fig 4 Mind Map of chapters 8–19, the Polymathic Knowledge areas. To make *Master Your Memory* even *more* memorable, why not colour each branch of the Mind Map as you complete each chapter?

memory matrices for any other lists that would be useful to you, and to make a habit of memorising at least one new list per year.

Should you wish to remember the matrix itself, the Basic One Hundred can be used to memorise each of the Key Words in the matrix, thus further using the system to memorise itself.

To get you off to a good start, it is recommended that you select from *Master Your Memory* at least two of the lists included. This will provide your brain with enough units of organised data to set your 'memory engine' on course for automatic growth! (*See Note, page 11.*)

Before you settle down to the task of further developing your extraordinary memory skills, the next chapter is intended to be a bridge between your knowledge and application. The chapter is a story about someone with a perfect memory. As you read it, check whether the Memory Principles and Techniques are being applied, and estimate what percentage of his brain you think the main character is using!

Onword

After you have read the chapter, plan your own memory development programme using SEM [3], and begin!

Memorising a Life:
the Story of Funes,
the Memorious

Critics are still trying to determine whether the following story by Jorge Luis Borges was a fabrication, a brilliant work of imagination, or true reportage. In view of what you have read so far, decide for yourself.

Is it possible? Did Funes really exist? Is the story true?

Funes, the Memorious

I remember him (I scarcely have the right to use this ghostly verb; only one man on earth deserved the right, and he is dead), I remember him with a dark passionflower in his hand, looking at it as no one has ever looked at such a flower, though they might look from the twilight of day until the twilight of night, for a whole life long. I remember him, his face immobile and Indian-like, and singularly *remote*, behind his cigarette. I remember (I believe) the strong delicate fingers of the plainsman who can braid leather. I remember, near those hands, a vessel in which to make maté tea, bearing the arms of the Banda Oriental;* I remember, in the window of the house, a yellow rush mat, and beyond, a vague marshy landscape. I remember clearly his voice, the deliberate, resentful nasal voice of the old Eastern Shore man, without the Italianate syllables of today, I did not see him more than three times; the last time, in 1887...

That all those who knew him should write something about him seems to me a very felicitous idea; my testimony may perhaps be

*The Eastern Shore (of the Uruguay River); now the Orient Republic of Uruguay. – *Editor's note.*

the briefest and without doubt the poorest, and it will not be the least impartial. The deplorable fact of my being an Argentinian will hinder me from falling into a dithyramb – an obligatory form in the Uruguay, when the theme is an Uruguayan.

Littérateur, slicker, Buenos Airean: Funes did not use these insulting phrases, but I am sufficiently aware that for him I represented these unfortunate categories. Pedro Leandlo Ipuche has written that Funes was a precursor of the superman, 'an untamed and vernacular Zarathustra'; I do not doubt it, but one must not forget, either, that he was a countryman from the town of Fray Bentos, with certain incurable limitations.

My first recollection of Funes is quite clear, I see him at dusk, some time in March or February of the year '84. That year, my father had taken me to spend the summer at Fray Bentos. I was on my way back from the farm in San Francisco with my cousin Bernardo Haedo. We came back singing, on horseback; and this last fact was not the only reason for my joy. After a sultry day, an enormous slate-grey storm had obscured the sky. It was driven on by a wind from the south; the trees were already tossing like madmen; and I had the apprehension (the secret hope) that the elemental downpour would catch us out in the open. We were running a kind of race with the tempest. We rode into a narrow lane which wound down between two enormously high brick footpaths. It had grown black of a sudden; I now heard rapid almost secret steps above; I raised my eyes and saw a boy running along the narrow, cracked path as if he were running along a narrow, broken wall. I remember the loose trousers, tight at the bottom, the hemp sandals; I remember the cigarette in the hard visage, standing out against the by now limitless darkness. Bernardo unexpectedly yelled to him: 'What's the time, Ireneo?' Without looking up, without stopping, Ireneo replied: 'In ten minutes it will be eight o'clock, child Bernardo Juan Francisco'. The voice was sharp, mocking.

I am so absentminded that the dialogue which I have just cited would not have penetrated my attention if it had not been repeated by my cousin, who was stimulated, I think, by a certain local pride and by a desire to show himself indifferent to the other's three-sided reply.

He told me that the boy above us in the pass was a certain Ireneo Funes, renowned for a number of eccentricities, such as that of having nothing to do with people and of always knowing the time, like a watch. He added that Ireneo was the son of Maria Clementine Funes, an ironing woman in the town, and that his father, some people said, was an 'Englishman' named O'Connor, a doctor in the salting fields, though some said the father was a horse-breaker, or scout, from the province of El Salto. Ireneo lived with his mother, at the edge of the country house of the Laurels.

In the years '85 and '86 we spent the summer in the city of Montevideo. We returned to Fray Bentos in '87. As was natural, I inquired after all my acquaintances, and finally, about 'the chronometer Funes'. I was told that he had been thrown by a wild horse at the San Francisco ranch, and that he had been hopelessly crippled. I remember the impression of uneasy magic which the news provoked in me: the only time I had seen him we were on horseback, coming from San Francisco, and he was in a high place; from the lips of my cousin Bernardo the affair sounded like a dream elaborated with elements out of the past. They told me that Ireneo did not move now from his cot, but remained with his eyes fixed on the backyard fig tree, or on a cobweb. At sunset he allowed himself to be brought to the window. He carried pride to the extreme of pretending that the blow which had befallen him was a good thing . . . Twice I saw him behind the iron gate which sternly delineated his eternal imprisonment: unmoving, once, his eyes closed; unmoving also, another time, absorbed in the contemplation of a sweet-smelling sprig of lavender cotton.

At the time I had begun, not without some ostentation, the methodical study of Latin. My valise contained the *De viris illustribus* of Lhomond, the *Thesaurus* of Quicherat, *Caesar's Commentaries,* and an odd-numbered volume of the *Historia Naturalis* of Pliny, which exceeded (and still exceeds) my modest talents as a Latinist. Everything is noised around in a small town; Ireneo, at his small farm on the outskirts, was not long in learning of the arrival of these anomalous books. He sent me a flowery, ceremonious letter, in which he recalled our encounter, unfortunately brief, 'on the seventh day of February of the year '84,' and alluded to the glorious services which Don Gregorio Haedo, my uncle, dead the same year, 'had rendered to the Two Fatherlands in the glorious campaign of Ituzaingó,' and he solicited the loan of any one of the volumes, to be accompanied by a dictionary 'for the better intelligence of the original text, for I do not know Latin as yet.' He promised to return them in good condition, almost immediately. The letter was perfect, very nicely constructed; the orthography was of the type sponsored by Andres Bello: *i* for *y*, *j* for *g*. At first I naturally suspected a jest. My cousins assured me it was not so, that these were the ways of Ireneo. I did not know whether to attribute to impudence, ignorance, or stupidity, the idea that the difficult Latin required no other instrument than a dictionary; in order fully to undeceive him I sent the *Gradus ad Parnassum* of Quicherat, and the Pliny.

On 14 February, I received a telegram from Buenos Aires telling me to return immediately, for my father was 'in no way well'. God forgive me, but the prestige of being the recipient of an urgent telegram, the desire to point out to all of Fray Bentos the contradiction between the negative form of the news and the positive adverb, the temptation to dramatise my sorrow as I feigned a virile stoicism, all no doubt distracted me from the possibility of anguish. As I packed my valise, I noticed that I was missing the *Gradus* and the volume of the *Historia Naturalis*. The *Saturn* was to weigh anchor on the morning of the next day; that night, after supper, I made my way to the house of Funes. Outside, I was surprised to find the night no less oppressive than the day.

Ireneo's mother received me at the modest ranch.

She told me that Ireneo was in the back room and that I should not be disturbed to find him in the dark, for he knew how to pass the dead hours without lighting the candle. I crossed the cobblestone patio, the small corridor; I came to the second patio. A great vine covered everything, so that the darkness seemed complete. Of a sudden I heard the high-pitched, mocking voice of Ireneo. The voice spoke in Latin; the voice (which came out of the obscurity) was reading, with obvious delight, a treatise or prayer or incantation. The Roman syllables resounded in the earthen patio; my suspicion made them seem undecipherable, interminable; afterwards, in the enormous dialogue of that night, I learned that they made up the first paragraph of the twenty-fourth chapter of the seventh book of the *Historia Naturalis*. The subject of this chapter is memory; the last words are *ut nihil non iisdem verbis redderetur auditum*.

Without the least change in his voice, Ireneo bade me come in. He was lying on the cot, smoking. It seems to me that I did not see his face until dawn; I seem to recall the momentary glow of the cigarette. The room smelled vaguely of dampness. I sat down, and repeated the story of the telegram and my father's illness.

I come now to the most difficult point in my narrative. For the entire story has no other point (the reader might as well know it by now) than this dialogue of almost a half-century ago. I shall not attempt to reproduce his words, now irrecoverable. I prefer truthfully to make a résumé of the many things Ireneo told me. The indirect style is remote and weak; I know that I sacrifice the effectiveness of my narrative; but let my readers imagine the nebulous sentences which clouded that night.

Ireneo began by enumerating, in Latin and Spanish, the cases of prodigious memory cited in the *Historia Naturalis:* Cyrus, king of the Persians, who could call every soldier in his armies by name; Mithridates Eupator, who administered justice in the twenty-two languages of his empire; Simoniedes, inventor of mnemotechny; Metrodorus, who practised the art of repeating faithfully what he heard once. With evident good faith Funes marvelled that such things should be considered marvellous. He told me that previous to the rainy afternoon when the blue-tinted horse threw him, he had been – like any Christian – blind, deaf-mute, somnambulistic, memoryless. (I tried to remind him of his precise perception of time, his memory for proper names; he paid no attention to me.) For nineteen years, he said, he had lived like a person in a dream: he looked without seeing, heard without hearing, forgot everything – almost everything. On falling from the horse, he lost consciousness; when he recovered it, the present was almost intolerable it was so rich and bright; the same was true of the most ancient and most trivial memories. A little later he realised that he was crippled. This fact scarcely interested him. He reasoned (or felt) that immobility was a minimum price to pay. And now, his perception and his memory were infallible.

We, in a glance, perceive three wine glasses on the table; Funes saw all the shoots, clusters, and grapes of the vine. He remembered the shapes of the clouds in the south at dawn on the 30th of April of 1882, and he could compare them in his recollection with the marbled grain in the design of a leatherbound book which he had seen only once, and with the lines in the spray which an oar raised in the Rio Negro on the eve of the battle of the Quebracho. These recollections were not simple; each visual image was linked to muscular sensations, thermal sensations, etc. He could reconstruct all his dreams, all his fancies. Two or three times he had reconstructed an entire day. He told me: *I have* more *memories in myself alone than all men have had since the world was a world.* And again: *My dreams are like your vigils.* And again, toward dawn: *My memory, sir, is like a garbage disposal.*

A circumference on a blackboard, a rectangular triangle, a rhomb, are forms which we can fully intuit; the same held true with Ireneo for the tempestuous mane of a stallion, a herd of cattle in a pass, the ever-changing flame or the innumerable ash, the many faces of a dead man during the course of a protracted wake. He could perceive I do not know how many stars in the sky.

These things he told me; neither then nor at any time later did they seem doubtful. In those days neither the cinema nor the phonograph yet existed; nevertheless, it seems strange, almost incredible, that no one should have experimented on Funes. The truth is that we all live by leaving behind; no doubt we all profoundly know that we are immortal and that sooner or later every man will do all things and know everything.

The voice of Funes, out of the darkness, continued. He told me that toward 1886 he had devised a new system of enumeration and that in a very few days he had gone beyond twenty-four thousand. He had not written it down, for what he once mediated would not be erased. The first stimulus to his work, I believe, had been his discontent with the fact that 'thirty-three Uruguayans' required two symbols and three words, rather than a single word and a single symbol. Later he applied his extravagant principle to the other numbers. In place of seven thousand thirteen, he would say (for example) *Máximo Perez;* in place of seven thousand fourteen, *The Train;* other numbers were *Luis Melián Lafinur, Olimar, Brimstone, Clubs, The Whale, Gas, The Cauldron, Napoleon, Agustín de Vedia.* In lieu of five hundred, he would say *nine.* Each word had a particular sign, a species of mark; the last were very complicated . . . I attempted to explain that this rhapsody of unconnected terms was precisely the contrary of a system of enumeration. I said that to say three hundred and sixty-five was to say three hundreds, six tens, five units: an analysis which does not exist in such numbers as *The Negro Tmoteo* or *The Flesh Blanket.* Funes did not understand me, or did not wish to understand me.

Locke, in the seventeenth century, postulated (and rejected) an impossible idiom in which each individual object, each stone, each bird and branch had an individual name; Funes had once projected an analogous idiom, but he had renounced it as being too general, too ambiguous. In effect, Funes not only remembered every leaf on every tree of every wood, but even every one of the times he had perceived or imagined it. He determined to reduce all of his past experience to some seventy thousand recollections, which he would later define numerically. Two considerations dissuaded him: the thought that the task was interminable and the thought that it was useless. He knew that at the hour of his death he would scarcely have finished classifying even all the memories of his childhood.

The two projects I have indicated (an infinite vocabulary for the natural series of numbers, and a usable mental catalogue of all the images of memory) are lacking in sense, but they reveal a certain stammering greatness. They allow us to make out dimly, or to infer, the dizzying world of Funes. He was, let us not forget, almost incapable of general, platonic ideas. It was not only difficult for him to understand that the generic term *dog* embraced so many unlike specimens of differing sizes and different forms; he was disturbed by the fact that a dog at three-fourteen (seen in profile) should have the same name as the dog at three-fifteen (seen from the front). His own face in the mirror, his own hands, surprised him on every occasion. Swift writes that the emperor of Lilliput could discern the movement of the minute hand; Funes could continuously make out the tranquil advances of corruption, of caries, of fatigue. He noted the progress of death, of moisture. He was the solitary and lucid spectator of a multiform world which was instantaneously and almost intolerably exact. Babylon, London, and New York have overawed the imagination of men with their ferocious splendour; no one, in those populous towers or upon those surging avenues, has felt the heat and pressure of a reality as indefatigable as that which day and night converged upon the unfortunate Ireneo in his humble South American farmhouse. It was very difficult for him to sleep. To sleep is to be abstracted from the world; Funes, on his back in his cot, in the shadows, imagined every crevice and every moulding of the various houses which surrounded him. (I repeat, the least important of his recollections was more minutely precise and more lively than our perception of a physical pleasure or a physical torment.) Toward the east, in a section which was not yet cut into blocks of homes, there were some new unknown houses. Funes imagined them black, compact, made of a single obscurity; he would turn his face in this direction in order to sleep. He would also imagine himself at the bottom of the river, being rocked and annihilated by the current.

Without effort, he had learned English, French, Portuguese, Latin. I suspect, nevertheless, that he was not very capable of thought. To think is to forget a difference, to generalise, to abstract. In the overly replete world of Funes there was nothing but details, almost contiguous details.

The equivocal clarity of dawn penetrated along the earthen patio.

Then it was that I saw the face of the voice which had spoken all through the night. Ireneo was nineteen years old; he had been born in 1868; he seemed as monumental as bronze, more ancient than

Egypt, anterior to the prophecies and the pyramids. It occurred to me that each one of my words (each one of my gestures) would live on in his implacable memory; I was benumbed by the fear of multiplying superfluous gestures.

Ireneo Funes died in 1889, of a pulmonary congestion.

1942   *Translated by* ANTHONY KERRIGAN

(Taken from *Fictions* by Jorge Luis Borges, published by J. Calder, London.)

The Artists 8

Leonardo da Vinci said, if you wish to develop an all round mind, make sure you 'study the Science of Art, and study the Art of Science'.

The great artists have spearheaded mankind's research into the nature of our perception. They have also recorded human history with an elegance at least equal to that of the poets, novelists, dramatists and literary historians. Knowing their names, birthplaces, dates of birth and death, and some of their famous works, places them, as you did with the Planets, in a context and perspective that allows you automatically and continually to learn more about them as you progress through life.

In memorising the great Artists, Composers and Writers, you might, for example, choose SEM^3 numbers from 1000 to 1300, if you had already used your first thousand. Let's assume that Leonardo da Vinci was your number 1020. Your SEM^3 Key Memory Image is the number 20 (NASA) joined with the Sound-image of Singing.

To remember that Leonardo was a high Renaissance (rebirth) inventor, one of his famous works being 'Virgin of the Rocks', you could imagine a beautiful dale in which he was sitting at an easel, painting the scene perfectly on a giant canvas while singing an operatic aria (to remind you that he was Italian). To remember Renaissance (rebirth) you could place a little baby by Leonardo's side helping him with his paints. At the end of the dale you could imagine a giant outcrop of rocks on which a beautiful virgin was trapped and calling for help (you might even make her a bit like the Mona Lisa). To remember the dates 1452 to 1519, you would take the numbers 4 = R, 5 = L, 2 = N; 5 = L, 1 = T or D, 9 = B, and make word images from them that related to da Vinci. For example, Renaissance Leading Naturalist; Leonardo Da Vinci's Burial. Apply these principles and examples to memorising whichever of the major knowledge matrices most appeals to you.

Information about each of the major European artists has been categorised under four headings to aid you both in speed of reference and ability to memorise: Name, Famous work and School.

Onword

Every time you see an advertisement for an art exhibition in future, the images and information pertaining to that exhibition and artist will add to your growing body of Art Knowledge, and will increase your knowledge of this most important area to your continuing advantage.

1 **Duccio di Buoninsegna**   1255–1318   Italian
   Famous work: Christ Entering Jerusalem
   (Cathedral Museum, Siena)
   School: Sienese, Pre-Renaissance

2 **Giotto**   1267–1337   Italian
   Famous work: The Lamentation
   (Fresco in Arena Chapel, Padua)
   School: Florentine, Pre-Renaissance

3 **Simone Martini**   1284–1344   Italian
   Famous work: The Annunciation (Uffizi Gallery, Florence)
   School: Sienese

4 **Jan van Eyck**   1385/90–1441   Dutch
   Famous work: Giovanni Arnolfini and his Bride
   (National Gallery, London)
   School: Flemish

5 **Fra Angelico**   1387–1455   Italian
   Famous work: The Annunciation
   (Monastery of San Marco, Florence)
   School: Florentine

6 Paolo Uccello   1397–1475   Italian
Famous work: The Battle of San Romano
(National Gallery, London)
School: Florentine

7 Roger van der Weyden   1399–1464   Flemish
Famous work: The Deposition (Prado, Madrid)
School: Flemish

8 Masaccio   1401–1428   Italian
Famous work: The Rendering of the Tribute Money
(Brancacci Chapel, Santa Maria del Carmine, Florence)
School: Florentine

9 Piero della Francesca   1410/20–1492   Italian
Famous work: The Resurrection
(Palazzo Cominale, Boreo San Sepolcro)
School: Umbrian

10 Giovanni Bellini   1430–1516   Italian
Famous work: The Madonna of the Meadow
(National Gallery, London)
School: Venetian

11 Andrea Mantegna   1431–1506   Italian
Famous work: Christ Praying in the Garden
(National Gallery, London)
School: Mantuan

12 Luca Signorelli   1441/50–1523   Italian
Famous work: Pan as God of Music
(Staatliche Museen, Berlin)
School: Umbrian

13 Sandro Botticelli   1445–1510   Italian
Famous work: The Birth of Venus (Uffizi Gallery, Florence)
School: Florentine

14 Hieronymus Bosch   1450–1516   Dutch
Famous work: The Garden of Earthly Delights
(Prado, Madrid)
School: Flemish

15 Leonardo da Vinci   1452–1519   Italian
Famous work: The Virgin of the Rocks (Louvre, Paris)
School: Florentine

16 Albrecht Dürer   1471–1528   German
Famous work: The Four Apostles (Pinakothek, Munich)
School: German

17 Michelangelo Buonarroti   1475–1564   Italian
Famous work: Sistine Chapel Ceiling (Vatican, Rome)
School: Florentine

18 Mathis Grünewald   1470/80–1528   German
Famous work: The Crucifixion, from the Isenheim
Altarpiece (Musée Unterlinden, Colmar)
School: German

19 Giorgione   1477–1510   Italian
Famous work: Fête Champêtre (Louvre, Paris)
School: Venetian

20 Raphael   1483–1520   Italian
Famous work: The School of Athens (Vatican, Rome)
School: Florentine

21 Titian   1487–1576   Italian
Famous work: The Death of Acteon
(National Gallery, London)
School: Venetian

22 Antonio Correggio   1489/94–1534   Italian
Famous work: Danae (Galleria Borghese, Rome)
School: Parma

23 Hans Holbein (The Younger)   1497–1543   German
Famous work: Portrait of Erasmus (Louvre, Paris)
School: German

24 Jacopo Tintoretto   1518–1594   Italian
Famous work: The Last Supper (Santa Marciola, Venice)
School: Venetian Mannerist

25 Pieter Bruegel (The Elder)   1520/30–1569   Flemish
Famous work: The Parable of the Blind
(Museo Nazionale, Naples)
School: Flemish

26 Paolo Veronese   1528–1588   Italian
Famous work: Christ in the House of Levi (Academy, Venice)
School: Venetian

27 El Greco   1541–1614   Greek
Famous work: The Assumption of the Virgin
(1577, Art Institute of Chicago)
School: Spanish (by adoption)

28 Annibale Carracci   1560–1609   Italian
Famous work: Hercules at the Crossroads
School: Bolognese, Classical

**29 Michelangelo Merisi
da Caravaggio**   1571–1610   Italian
Famous work: The Supper at Emmaus
(National Gallery, London)
School: Independent Tenebrist

30 Sir Peter Paul Rubens   1577–1640   Flemish
Famous work: Descent from the Cross (Antwerp Cathedral)
School: Flemish, Baroque

31 Frans Hals   1581–1666   Dutch
Famous work: The Laughing Cavalier
School: Dutch

32 Georges de la Tour   1593–1652   French
Famous work: The Adoration of the Shepherds
(Louvre, Paris)
School: Lorraine

33 Nicolas Poussin   1595–1665   French
Famous work: Rape of the Sabine Women
(Metropolitan Museum, New York)
School: French, worked mainly in Rome, Classical

34 Francisco de Zurbárán   1598–1664   Spanish
Famous work: St Francis of Assisi (Lyon Museum)
School: Spanish

35 Sir Anthony van Dyck   1599–1641   Flemish
Famous work: Charles I of England (The King Hunting),
(Louvre, Paris)
School: Flemish

**36 Diego Rodriguez de Silva
y Velasquez**   1599–1660   Spanish
Famous work: Las Meninas (Prado, Madrid)
School: Spanish

37 Gelle Claude (Claude Lorraine)   1600–1682   French
Famous work: The Embarkation of the Queen of Sheba
(National Gallery, London)
School: French, Romantic Classicist

38 Bartolome Esteban Murillo   1617/18–1682   Spanish
Famous work: The Immaculate Conception
(Seville Museum)
School: Spanish

39 Harmensz van Rijn Rembrandt   1606–1669   Dutch
Famous work: The Night Watch (Rijksmuseum, Amsterdam)
School: Dutch

40 Jacob van Ruisdael   1628/29–1682   Dutch
Famous work: The Bleaching Ground
(National Gallery, London)
School: Dutch

41 Jan Vermeer   1632–1675   Dutch
Famous work: The Music Lesson (Queen's Gallery, London)
School: Dutch

42 Jean Antoine Watteau   1684–1721   French
Famous work: The Pilgrimage to the Island of Cythera
(Louvre, Paris)
School: French

43 Giovanni Batista Tiepolo   1696–1770   Italian
Famous work: Antony and Cleopatra Frescoes
(Palazzo Labia, Venice)
School: Venetian

44 William Hogarth   1697–1764   English
Famous work: Marriage à la Mode
(National Gallery, London)
School: English

45 (Giovanni) Antonio Canaletto   1697–1768   Italian
Famous work: The Basin of San Marco on Ascension Day
(National Gallery, London)
School: Venetian

46 Jean Baptiste Simeon Chardin   1699–1779   French
Famous work: Kitchen Still Life
(Museum of Fine Arts, Boston)
School: French

47 François Boucher   1703–1770   French
Famous work: The Triumph of Venus (Stockholm Museum)
School: French, Rococo

48 Sir Joshua Reynolds   1723–1792   English
Famous work: Mrs Siddons as the Tragic Muse
(Huntingdon Library, San Marino, California)
School: English

49 George Stubbs   1724–1806   English
Famous work: White Horse Frightened by a Lion
(Walker Art Gallery, Liverpool)
School: English

50 Thomas Gainsborough   1727–1788   English
Famous work: Mr and Mrs Andrews
(National Gallery, London)
School: English

51 Jean Honoré Fragonard   1732–1806   French
Famous work: The Pursuit (Frick Collection, New York)
School: French, Rococo

52 Joseph Wright of Derby   1734–1797   English
Famous work: Experiment on a Bird in an Air Pump
(Tate Gallery, London)
School: English

53 Francisco de Goya y Lucientes   1746–1828   Spanish
Famous work: The Third of May (Prado, Madrid)
School: Spanish

54 Jacques Louis David   1748–1825   French
Famous work: Death of Marat
(Royal Museum of Fine Art, Brussels)
School: French, Neo-classical

55 William Blake   1757–1827   English
Famous work: Dante Meeting Beatrice in Paradise
(Tate Gallery, London)
School: English

56 Caspar David Friedrich   1774–1840   German
Famous work: Man and Woman Gazing at the Moon
(National Galerie, Berlin)
School: German Romantic

57 Joseph Mallord William Turner   1775–1851   English
Famous work: Rain, Steam and Speed
(National Gallery, London)
School: English

58 John Constable   1776–1837   English
Famous work: The Haywain (National Gallery, London)
School: English

59 Jean Auguste Dominique Ingres   1780–1867   French
Famous work: Le Bain Turc (Louvre, Paris)
School: French, Neo-classical

60 John Sell Cotman   1782–1842   English
Famous work: Chirk Aqueduct (Victoria and Albert Museum)
School: English, Norwich

61 Théodore Géricault   1791–1824   French
Famous work: The Raft of the Medusa (Louvre, Paris)
School: French, Romantic

62 Jean Baptiste Camille Corot   1796–1875   French
Famous work: Souvenir de Morte Fontaine (Louvre, Paris)
School: French

63 Eugene Delacroix   1798–1863   French
Famous work: Liberty on the Barricades
School: French, Romantic

64 Jean François Millet   1814–1875   French
Famous work: The Angelus (Louvre, Paris)
School: French, Romantic

65 Gustave Courbet   1819–1877   French
Famous work: Good Morning, Monsieur Courbet
(Musee Fabre, Montpellier)
School: French, Realist

66 William Holman Hunt   1827–1910   English
Famous work: The Light of the World
(Keble College, Oxford)
School: English, Pre-Raphaelite Brotherhood

67 Arnold Bocklin   1827–1901   Swiss
Famous work: Island of the Dead
(Metropolitan Museum, New York)
School: Swiss, Romantic

68 Camille Pissaro   1831–1903   French
Famous work: The Red Roofs (Louvre, Paris)
School: French Impressionist (Landscape)

69 Edouard Manet   1832–1883   French
Famous work: A Bar at the Folies-Bergère
(Courtauld Institute, London)
School: French, Urban Impressionist

70 Edgar Degas   1834–1917   French
Famous work: The Dancing Class (Musée d'Orsay, Paris)
School: French, Urban Impressionist

71 Paul Cézanne   1839–1906   French
Famous work: Mont Sainte-Victoire (Museum of Art,
Philadelphia)
School: French, Post Impressionist

72 Odilon Redon   1840–1916   French
Famous work: Silence (Museum of Modern Art, New York)
School: French Symbolist

73 Claude Monet   1840–1926   French
Famous work: Water Lilies Series (Louvre, Paris)
School: French Impressionist

74 Pierre-Auguste Renoir   1841–1919   French
Famous work: Ball at the Moulin de la Galette
(Musée d'Orsay, Paris)
School: French Impressionist

75 Paul Gauguin   1848–1903   French
Famous work: Riders on the Beach
(Folkwang Museum, Essen)
School: French, Post Impressionist

76 Vincent van Gogh   1853–1890   Dutch
Famous work: Sunflowers (National Gallery, London)
School: French, Post Impressionist

77 Georges Seurat   1859–1891   French
Famous work: The Bathers at Asnières
(National Gallery, London)
School: French, Pointillist

78 Walter Richard Sickert   1860–1942   English
Famous work: The Eldorado, Paris
(University of Birmingham)
School: Camden Town Group (Post Impressionist)

79 Edvard Munch   1863–1944   Norwegian
Famous work: The Scream (National Gallery, Oslo)
School: Norwegian, Precursor of Expressionism

80 Wassily Kandinsky   1866–1944   Russian
Famous work: Improvisation No. 30 (Cannons)
(Art Institute of Chicago)
School: Der Blaue Reiter (The Blue Horseman), Abstract

81 Pierre Bonnard   1867–1947   French
Famous work: Coffee (Tate Gallery, London)
School: Intimist

82 Henri Matisse   1869–1954   French
Famous work: Red Studio
(Museum of Modern Art, New York)
School: Fauve

83 Giacomo Balla   1871–1958   Italian
Famous work: Dog on a Leash
(A. Congere Goodyear, New York)
School: Italian Futurist

84 Georges Rouault   1871–1958   French
Famous work: The Apprentice (Musée d'Art Moderne, Paris)
School: School of Paris, Independent Expressionist

85 Piet Mondrian   1872–1944   Dutch
Famous work: Broadway Boogie Woogie
(Museum of Modern Art, New York)
School: De Stijl, Neoplasticism, Abstract

86 Paul Klee   1879–1940   German/Swiss
Famous work: Landscape with Yellow Birds
(Doetsch-Benzinger Collection, Basel)
School: Associated with Der Blaue Reiter, Independent

87 Fernand Léger   1881–1955   French
Famous work: Les Fumeurs (Smokers)
(Guggenheim Museum, New York)
School: Cubist

88 Pablo Ruiz y Picasso   1881–1973   Spanish
Famous work: Guernica (Prado, Madrid)
School: Cubist

89 Georges Braque   1882–1963   French
Famous work: Studio IX (Maeght Collection, Paris)
School: Cubist

90 Max Beckman   1884–1950   German
Famous work: Departure
(Museum of Modern Art, New York)
School: Expressionist

91 Percy Wyndham Lewis   1884–1957   English
Famous work: Portrait of Edith Sitwell
(Tate Gallery, London)
School: Vorticist (English Branch of Cubism/Futurism)

92 Robert Delaunay   1885–1941   French
Famous work: Window on the City No. 4
(Guggenheim Museum, New York)
School: School of Paris, Orphist

93 Juan Gris   1887–1927   Spanish
Famous work: Still Life in Front of an Open Window
(Arenburg Collection, Philadelphia Museum of Art)
School: Cubist

94 Marc Chagall   1887–1985   Russian
Famous work: I and the Village
(Museum of Modern Art, New York)
School: School of Paris, Independent Fantasist

95 Giorgio de Chirico   1888–1978   Italian
Famous work: Enigma of Arrival (Private Collection, Paris)
School: Italian Metaphysical

96 Paul Nash   1889–1946   English
Famous work: Totesmeer (Tate Gallery, London)
School: English Surrealist

97 Max Ernst   1891–1976   German
Famous work: Swamp Angel
(Macpherson Collection, Rome)
School: Surrealist

98 Stanley Spencer   1891–1959   English
Famous work: The Murals at Burghclere Chapel
School: Independent, Religious

99 René Magritte   1898–1967   Belgian
Famous work: The False Mirror (Museum of Modern Art,
New York)
School: Surrealist

100 Salvador Dali   1904–1989   Spanish
Famous work: The Persistence of Memory
(Museo Nacional Centro de Arte Reina Sophia, Madrid)
School: Surrealist

The
Composers

As artists record the visual history of the human race, so the great composers record the aural/musical history. Sound, as the basis for one of your five senses, hearing, is automatically a major memory device. It is also one of the areas of mental skill that is essential for the development of the Master Memory skill of synaesthesia – the blending of the senses for the enhancement of each and the correlative increase in mental skills, especially creativity and memory.

Once you have organised and memorised, using SEM^3, the following list of composers and the major information about them, you will have created a foundation of musical knowledge that will allow your brain *automatically* to build multiple associations around each composer and each composer's music, and rapidly to integrate those into a growing fabric of delightful and spirit-enhancing knowledge.

When you hear for example on BBC Radio 3, that Smetana was originally known for his astounding energy and enthusiasm, that his two children died at an early age, and that he lost his life to the most debilitating disease, causing the physical disintegration of his brain, and yet that he still composed and recorded in intricate detail the nature of his decline and the nature of its effect on his memory, you will listen to his music with greater understanding and compassion, and similarly will know more about the historical times in which he lived.

Onword

By using SEM3 in this way, you will be exploring, with the great historical and current musical brains, the human race's search, through the medium of sound, for an increasing understanding of its own nature.

1 Philippe de Vitry   1291–1361   French
Famous work: Impudenter circumivi/ Virtutibus
Style: Secular and of the Ars Nova
Era: Middle Ages

2 Guillaume de Machaut   1300–1377   French
Famous work: Messe de Notre Dame
Style: Sacred and secular
Notes: Well-respected statesman, cleric and poet
Era: Middle Ages

3 Francesco Landini   1325–1397   Italian
Famous work: Ecco la primavera
Style: Secular
Notes: Blind from childhood
Era: Middle Ages

4 John Dunstable   1390–1453   English
Famous work: O Rosa Bella
Style: Sacred and secular
Notes: Well known for 'singability' of his music
Era: Middle Ages

5 Gilles de Bins Binchois   1400–1460   Franco-Flemish
Famous work: Filles à marier
Style: Sacred and secular
Era: Renaissance

6 Guillaume Dufay   1400–1474   Franco-Flemish
Famous work: Se la face ay pale
Style: Sacred and secular
Era: Renaissance

7 Johannes Ockeghem   1410–1497   Franco-Flemish
Famous work: Missa cuiusvi toni
Style: Sacred and secular
Era: Renaissance

8 Josquin Desprez   1440–1521   Franco-Flemish
Famous work: Ave Maria
Style: Sacred and secular
Era: Renaissance

9 Heinrich Isaac   1450–1517   Flemish
Famous work: Choralis constantinus
Style: Sacred and secular vocal music
Era: Renaissance

10 Andrea Gabrieli   1510–1586   Italian
Famous work: Magnificat for 3 choirs and orchestra
Style: Sacred and madrigals
Notes: Introduced technique 'Cori spezzati' (spaced choirs)
Era: Renaissance

11 Giovanni Pierluigi da Palestrina   1525–1594   Italian
Famous work: Missa Papae Marcelli
Style: Sacred and secular vocal music
Era: Renaissance

12 Orlande de Lassus   1532–1594   Franco-Flemish
Famous work: Alma redemptoris mater
Style: Sacred and secular vocal music
Era: Renaissance

13 William Byrd   1543–1623   English
Famous work: Sing Joyfully/Ave Verum Corpus
Style: Sacred and secular choral music, vocal chamber
music, instrumental and keyboard music
Notes: Described as 'Father of British Music'
Era: Renaissance

14 Giulio Caccini   1545–1618   Italian
Famous work: Toccate d'Intavolature di Cimbale e Organo
Style: Le Nuove Musiche
Era: Baroque

15 Tomás Luis de Victoria   1548–1611   Spanish
Famous work: Mass Laetatus Sum
Style: Songs in new styles
Era: Renaissance

16 Luca Marenzio   1553–1599   Italian
Famous work: Dolorosi martir
Style: Secular vocal music and sacred vocal music
Era: Renaissance

17 Giovanni Gabrieli   1555–1612   Italian
Famous work: Canzon XIII
Style: Sacred vocal music, instrumental music and secular
vocal music
Era: Renaissance

18 Thomas Morley   1557–1602   English
Famous work: Now Is the Month of Maying
Style: Secular and sacred vocal music, instrumental music
Notes: Specialised in Ballett Madrigals (light form of madrigal)
Era: Renaissance

19 Carlo Gesualdo   1560–1613   Italian
Famous work: Deh, coprite il bel seno
Style: Secular and sacred vocal music
Era: Renaissance

20 John Bull   1562–1628   English
Famous work: Fantasia
Style: Keyboard composer
Era: Renaissance

21 John Dowland   1563–1626   English
Famous work: In darkness let mee dwell
Style: Secular vocal, instrumental music
Era: Renaissance

22 Claudio Monteverdi   1567–1643   Italian
Famous works: Madrigals of Love and War, Il ritorno d'Ulisse
in patria (The return of Ulysses to his country)
Style: Secular vocal, sacred vocal, madrigals, operas
Era: Renaissance/Baroque

23 Thomas Weelkes   1575–1623   English
Famous work: As Vesta was from Latmos Hill descending
Style: Madrigals, sacred vocal and instrumental
Era: Renaissance

24 Orlando Gibbons   1583–1625   English
Famous works: This is the Record of John, The Silver Swan
Style: Vocal, sacred choral, keyboard and instrumental music
Era: Renaissance

25 Girolamo Frescobaldi   1583–1643   Italian
Famous work: Capriccio sopra la battaglia
Style: Vocal and keyboard music
Notes: Known as 'A giant among organists'
Era: Baroque

26 Heinrich Schütz   1585–1672   German
Famous works: St Matthew's Passion, Christmas Oratorio
Style: Secular and sacred vocal music
Era: Baroque

27 Francesco Cavalli   1602–1676   Italian
Famous work: Ercole Amante (Hercules the Lover)
Style: Secular vocal
Era: Baroque

28 Giacomo Carissimi   1605–1674   Italian
Famous work: The Representation of the Body and Soul
Style: Sacred musical dramas
Era: Baroque

29 Jean-Baptiste Lully   1632–1687   Italian
Famous work: L'amour médecin
Style: Sacred choral music, comedy ballet, operas, ballets and dance music
Era: Baroque

30 Dietrich Buxtehude   1637–1707   Danish
Famous work: Oratorios, cantatas, organ music
Style: Invented 'musica recitativa'
Notes: Began idea of evening music, public concerts in churches and known as great influence on Bach
Era: Baroque

31 Arcangelo Corelli   1653–1713   Italian
Famous work: Christmas Concerto
Style: Church sonatas
Era: Baroque

32 Henry Purcell   1659–1695   English
Famous works: My heart is inditing, Fantasia upon One Note
Style: Secular and sacred choral music, instrumental and
keyboard music
Era: Baroque

33 Alessandro Scarlatti   1660–1725   Italian
Famous work: Le Teodora augusta
Style: Sacred and secular, choral and vocal music, operas,
instrumental music
Era: Baroque

34 François Couperin   1668–1733   French
Famous work: Concerts Royaux
Style: Keyboard music especially harpsichord, chamber
music, sacred and secular vocal music
Era: Baroque

35 Antonio Vivaldi   1678–1741   Italian
Famous work: The Four Seasons
Style: Concertos, operas, sacred choral music and chamber
music
Era: Baroque

36 Georg Philipp Telemann   1681–1767   German
Famous work: Musique de table
Style: Progressive composer
Era: Baroque

37 Jean-Philippe Rameau   1683–1764   French
Famous work: Hippolyte et Aricie
Style: Operas, keyboard music, chamber music,
sacred choral music
Era: Baroque

38 Johann Sebastian Bach   1685–1750   German
Famous work: St John's Passion
Style: Sacred choral, secular vocal, orchestral chamber
music, keyboard music, organ music
Era: Baroque

39 Domenico Scarlatti   1685–1757   Italian
Famous work: Essercizi per Gravicembalo
Style: Keyboard, sacred choral, instrumental and operas
Era: Baroque

40 George Frideric Handel   1685–1759
German/English
Famous work: Water Music
Style: Operas, oratorios, sacred vocal, secular vocal,
orchestral, chamber and keyboard music
Era: Baroque

41 Christoph Willibald Gluck   1714–1787   German
Famous works: Don Juan, Orfeo ed Euridice
Style: Operas, ballet, songs, sacred vocal and chamber music
Era: Classical

42 Carl Philip Emanuel Bach   1714–1788   German
Famous work: Rondo in E Flat
Style: Keyboard, orchestral, chamber and choral music
Era: Classical

43 Franz Joseph Haydn   1732–1809   Austrian
Famous work: The London Symphony
Style: Symphonies, keyboard and chamber music, operas,
oratorios, choral music
Era: Classical

44 Johann Christian Bach   1735–1782   German
Famous work: Concerted Symphony in E flat
Style: Orchestral, chamber, organ, keyboard, operas and
sacred music
Era: Classicai

45 Luigi Boccherini   1743–1805   Italian
Famous work: String Quintet in E major, Opus 13 No. 5
Style: Chamber music, symphonies and concertos, opera
and sacred music
Era: Classical

46 Muzio Clementi   1752–1832   Italian
Famous work: Minuetto pastorale in D
Style: Composed for piano
Notes: Known as 'Father of pianoforte'
Era: Classical

47 Wolfgang Amadeus Mozart   1756–1791   Austrian
Famous work: The Magic Flute, Don Giovanni
Style: Operas, symphonies, concertos, choral music,
chambermusic, piano music, vocal music
Era: Classical

48 Ignace Pleyel   1757–1831   Austrian
Famous works: Sinfonies Concertantes
Style: Symphonies, chamber music
Era: Classical

49 Ludwig van Beethoven   1770–1827   German
Famous works: Pastoral Symphony, Fidelio
Style: Symphonies, concertos, choral music, piano music,
string quartets, chamber music, songs, opera
Notes: Radically transformed all the musical forms with
which he worked
Era: Classical

50 Carl Maria von Weber   1786–1826   German
Famous works: The Freeshooter, Invitation to the Dance
Style: Operas, orchestral music, piano music,
incidental music
Era: Romantic

51 Gioacchino Rossini   1792–1868   Italian
Famous works: Barber of Seville, William Tell
Style: Operas, sacred choral music, secular and
chamber music
Era: Romantic

52 Franz Schubert   1797–1828   Austrian
Famous works: Beautiful Maid of the Mill, The Trout Quintet
Style: Songs, orchestral, chamber, piano and operas
Notes: Died when only 31 years old
Era: Romantic

53 Vincenzo Bellini   1801–1835   Italian
Famous work: I Puritani
Style: Vocal, opera, songs and instrumental music
Era: Romantic

54 Hector Berlioz   1803–1869   French
Famous works: Symphonie Fantastique, Romeo et Juliette
Style: Opera, orchestral symphonies, sacred choral music,
secular choral music, vocal music
Era: Romantic

55 Felix Mendelssohn   1809–1847   German
Famous works: A Midsummer Night's Dream, The Hebrides
Style: Orchestral music, symphonies, chamber music, piano music, sacred choral music
Era: Romantic

56 Frédéric Chopin   1810–1849   Polish
Famous work: The Etudes
Style: Piano music, orchestral music, chamber music
Era: Romantic

57 Robert Schumann   1810–1856   German
Famous works: A Woman's Love and Life, Scenes from Faust
Style: Song, piano music, orchestral, chamber, opera and choral music
Era: Romantic

58 Franz Liszt   1811–1886   Hungarian
Famous works: The Hungarian Rhapsodies, Faust Symphony
Style: Orchestral music, piano music, choral music
Era: Romantic

59 Richard Wagner   1813–1883   German
Famous work: The Flying Dutchman
Style: Operas, orchestral music, songs
Era: Romantic

60 Giuseppe Verdi   1813–1901   Italian
Famous works: Rigoletto, Requiem
Style: Operas, sacred choral, secular choral, chamber music
Era: Romantic

61 Bedrich Smetana   1824–1884   Czechoslovak
Famous works: The Bartered Bride, Vltava
Style: Symphonic poems, chamber music and opera
Era: Turn of 19th Century

62 Anton Bruckner   1824–1896   Austrian
Famous work: Te Deum
Style: Symphonies, choral music, chamber music
Era: Turn of 19th Century

63 Alexander Borodin   1833–1887   Russian
Famous work: Prince Igor
Style: Symphonies and operas
Era: Turn of 19th Century

64 Johannes Brahms   1833–1897   German
Famous works: Hungarian Dance, Tragic Overture, German Requiem
Style: Orchestral, chamber music, piano music, choral music, songs
Era: Romantic

65 Modest Mussorgsky   1839–1881   Russian
Famous work: Sunless
Style: Operas, orchestral, songs and piano music
Era: Turn of 19th Century

66 Pyotr Ilyich Tchaikovsky   1840–1893   Russian
Famous works: Sleeping Beauty, The Nutcracker
Style: Operas, ballets, choral music, symphonies, chamber music
Era: Turn of 19th Century

67 Antonin Dvorak   1841–1904   Czechoslovak
Famous works: New World Symphony, The American Quartet
Style: Orchestral music, symphonies, operas, chamber music, choral music
Era: Turn of 19th Century

68 Nikolay Rimsky-Korsakov   1844–1908   Russian
Famous work: The Snow Maiden
Style: Operas, orchestral works
Era: Turn of 19th Century

69 Leos Janacek   1854–1928   Czechoslovak
Famous work: The Cunning Little Vixen
Style: Operas, choral, vocal, orchestral, chamber music
Era: Turn of 19th Century

70 Edward Elgar   1857–1934   English
Famous works: Pomp and Circumstance, Enigma Variations, The Apostles
Style: Orchestral, choral, chamber, songs, piano, incidental
Era: Turn of 19th Century

71 Giacomo Puccini   1858–1924   Italian
Famous works: La Bohème, Madame Butterfly
Style: Operas, choral music
Era: Turn of 19th Century

72 Hugo Wolf   1860–1903   Austrian
Famous work: Der Corregidor
Style: Songs, opera, orchestral, chamber music
Era: Turn of 19th Century

73 Gustav Mahler   1860–1911   Austrian
Famous works: The Resurrection, Songs of the Wayfarer,
The Boy's Magic Horn
Style: Symphonies, songs, choral music
Era: Turn of 19th Century

74 Claude Debussy   1862–1918   French
Famous works: Prélude à l'Après-midi d'un Faune, La Mer
Style: Orchestral, ballet, piano, chamber music
Era: Turn of 19th Century

75 Richard Strauss   1864–1949   German
Famous works: The Cavalier of the Rose, A Woman without
a Shadow
Style: Orchestral, operas, choral music, songs
Era: Turn of 19th Century

76 Jean Sibelius   1865–1957   Finnish
Famous works: Tone Poem en Saga, Night Ride and Sunrise,
The Tempest
Style: Orchestral, incidental, choral, chamber
Era: Turn of 19th Century

77 Ralph Vaughan Williams   1872–1958   British
Famous works: Pastoral Symphony, Fantasia on
Greensleeves
Style: Operas, ballets, orchestral music, incidental, vocal,
chamber music
Era: Modern Times

78 Sergei Rachmaninov   1873–1943   Russian
Famous works: Rhapsody on a Theme of Paganini for Piano
and Orchestra, The Bells
Style: Orchestral, piano and choral
Era: Turn of 19th Century

79 Arnold Schoenberg   1874–1951   Austrian
Famous works: The Blessed Hand, The Transfigured Knight
Style: Operas, choral, orchestral, chamber and vocal
Era: Modern Times

80 Charles Ives   1874–1954   American
Famous works: The Circus Band, Three Places in New England, The Unanswered Question
Style: Orchestral, choral, chamber and piano
Era: Modern Times

81 Maurice Ravel   1875–1937   French
Famous works: Rapsodie Espagnole, Mother Goose
Style: Orchestral, piano, chamber music, song
Era: Turn of 19th Century

82 Manuela de Falla   1876–1946   Spanish
Famous works: The Three-cornered Hat, Atlantida
Style: Opera, ballet, choral and piano
Era: Modern Times

83 Béla Bartók   1881–1945   Hungarian
Famous works: Duke Bluebeard's Castle, The Wooden Prince, The Miraculous Mandarin
Style: Operas, ballets, orchestral, chamber and piano music
Era: Modern Times

84 Igor Stravinsky   1882–1971   Russian
Famous works: The Firebird, The Rite of Spring, Orpheus, The Soldier's Tale
Style: Operas, ballets, orchestral music, choral music
Era: Modern Times

85 Anton Webern   1883–1945   Austrian
Famous works: Passacaglia, Das Augenlicht
Style: Orchestral, choral, chamber and vocal
Era: Modern Times

86 Edgard Varèse   1883–1965   French/American
Famous works: Amériques, Hyperprism
Style: Orchestral, vocal, instrumental and electronic
Era: Modern Times

87 Alban Berg   1885–1935   Austrian
Famous works: Wozzeck, Lulu
Style: Opera, orchestral, chamber music, songs, piano music
Era: Modern Times

88 Louis Durey   1888–1979   French
Famous work: Le Printemps au fond de la mer
Style: Opera, instrumental and vocal music
Notes: One of 'Les Six'
Era: Modern Times

89 Sergei Prokofiev   1891–1953   Ukrainian
Famous works: The Gambler, War and Peace,
Romeo and Juliet
Style: Opera, ballets, orchestral, choral, chamber music,
piano music
Era: Modern Times

90 Darius Milhaud   1892–1974   French
Famous work: Les Malheurs d'Orphée
Style: Orchestral, choral, chamber and keyboard music
Notes: One of 'Les Six'
Era: Modern Times

91 Germaine Tailleferre   1892–1983   French
Famous work: 6 Chansons Françaises
Style: Opera, instrumental and vocal music
Notes: One of 'Les Six'
Era: Modern Times

92 Arthur Honegger   1892–1955   French
Famous work: Le Roi David
Style: Opera, ballet, orchestral and vocal music
Notes: One of 'Les Six'
Era: Modern Times

93 Paul Hindemith   1895–1963   German
Famous works: Matthias The Painter, The Four
Temperaments
Style: Operas, ballets, orchestral, chamber, piano, organ,
vocal, choral
Era: Modern Times

94 Carl Orff   1895–1982   German
Famous work: Carmina Burana
Style: Cantatas
Era: Modern Times

95 Henry Cowell   1897–1965   American
Famous works: Synchrony, Hymn and Fuguing Tune, Mosaic
Style: Orchestral, instrumental, piano
Era: Modern Times

96 Francis Poulenc   1899–1963   French
Famous works: A Sonata for Two Clarinets, Dialogues des Carmélites
Style: Opera, instrumental and choral music
Notes: Leader of 'Les Six'
Era: Modern Times

97 Georges Auric   1899–1983   French
Famous works: Les Facheux, The Birds
Style: Opera, instrumental and choral music
Notes: One of 'Les Six'
Era: Modern Times

98 Kurt Weill   1900–1950   German
Famous works: The Threepenny Opera, The Knickerbocker Holiday, The Rise and Fall of the City of Mahagonny
Style: Opera, ballet, orchestral, choral and chamber
Era: Modern Times

99 Dmitri Shostakovich   1906–1975   Russian
Famous works: The First of May, Leningrad, The Nose
Style: Orchestral, operas, chamber music and piano
Era: Modern Times

100 Benjamin Britten   1913–1976   British
Famous works: The Turn of the Screw, A Midsummer Night's Dream, Variations on a Theme of Frank Bridge, Spring Symphony
Style: Operas, church, orchestral, choral and chamber
Era: Modern Times

The Writers 10

Writers are more than simply clever users of words. They may be more accurately described as investigators of *all* fields of human knowledge, using words as their major investigative tool.

When you explore the world of literature, you also explore the worlds of psychology, geography, philosophy, history, astronomy, economics, mathematics, politics, biology, physics, exploration, imagination and fantasy.

Thus, as you build up your Master Memory Matrix of the great writers, you will be simultaneously extending a multiplicity of associative grappling hooks into all realms of human knowledge. With every author and literary work you come to know, your ability to link with every other author and every other work will increase.

Onword

This increase in knowledge will have as its automatic companions an increase in your speed of learning and an increase in your enjoyment of language, literature and life.

1 **Geoffrey Chaucer**   1340–1400   British
Famous work: The Canterbury Tales
Educated: London
Notes: Known as the 'Father of English Literature'

2 **Edmund Spenser**   1552–1599   British
Famous works: The Faerie Queene, Colin Clout's Come Home Againe
Educated: Merchant Taylors School, Northampton, then Cambridge
Notes: Often called 'Father of the English Fairytale'

3 **Sir Walter Raleigh**   1552–1618   British
Famous works: The History of the World, The Discoverie of the Large, Rich and Beautiful Empyre of Guiana
Educated: Oxford (Law)
Notes: An explorer and adventurer who led expeditions to America and South America. He had an enquiring mind and an uncommon literary ability

4 **Francis Bacon (Lord Verulam)**   1561–1626   British
Famous work: The Advancement of Learning
Educated: Trinity College, Cambridge (Law)
Notes: Had unquenchable curiosity about nature of the world and behaviour of his fellow men

5 **William Shakespeare**   1564–1616   British
Famous works: Othello, King Lear, Macbeth, Antony and Cleopatra, etc.
Educated: Holy Trinity Church, Stratford
Notes: Most prolific period 1604–1608. It is said of him that 'he is not of an age but for all time'

6 **Christopher Marlowe**   1564–1593   British
Famous work: The Passionate Shepherd
Educated: Corpus Christi College, Cambridge
Notes: Died from stabbing during fight with friends while gambling on backgammon

7 **John Donne**   1572–1631   British
Famous works: Devotions, Elegies and Sonnets
Educated: Oxford and Cambridge
Notes: One of the Metaphysical poets; became Dean of St Paul's in 1621 and wrote 160 sermons

8 Ben Jonson   1572–1637   British
Famous works: Volpone, Bartholomew Fayre, Timber
Educated: Westminster School
Notes: Leader of new generation of poets known as
'The Tribe of Ben'

9 John Milton   1608–1674   British
Famous works: Paradise Lost, On His Blindness, Il Penseroso
Educated: Christ's College Cambridge
Notes: The Civil War diverted his energies to the
parliamentary and political struggle. Wrote Paradise Lost
and On His Blindness after he had become blind

10 John Bunyan   1628–1688   British
Famous works: The Pilgrim's Progress, Grace Abounding
Educated: Village school, Elstow
Notes: He wrote The Pilgrim's Progress while imprisoned
for 12 years for unlicensed preaching

11 John Dryden   1631–1700   British
Famous works: Marriage à la Mode, The Rehearsal
Educated: Westminster School and Trinity College,
Cambridge
Notes: Poet Laureate in 1668

12 Samuel Pepys   1633–1703   British
Famous work: Diary
Educated: St Paul's School and Magdalene College, Cambridge
Notes: Diary not deciphered until 1825

13 Daniel Defoe   1660–1731   British
Famous works: Robinson Crusoe
Educated: Stoke Newington Academy
Notes: Most prolific after age of 60; dubbed 'founder of
English journalism'

14 Jonathan Swift   1667–1745   British
Famous work: Gulliver's Travels
Educated: Kilkenny School and Trinity College, Dublin
Notes: From age 23 suffered from Ménière's Disease

15 Joseph Addison   1672–1719   British
Famous work: Cato
Educated: Charterhouse School and Magdalen College,
Oxford
Notes: Member of Parliament

16 George Berkeley   1685–1753   Irish
Famous works: An Essay Towards a New Theory of Vision, Alciphron
Educated: Trinity College, Dublin
Notes: First published works were tracts on mathematics, written in Latin

17 Alexander Pope   1688–1744   British
Famous works: The Rape of the Lock and translations of The Iliad and Odyssey
Educated: Self-educated
Notes: Suffered from ill-health most of his life

18 Samuel Richardson   1689–1761   British
Famous works: Pamela, Clarissa
Educated: Grew up in poverty, education sketchy
Notes: Obsessed with sex, which led to the popularity of his writing. Regarded as 'one of the founders of the modern novel'

19 Benjamin Franklin   1706–1790   American
Famous works: Observation on the Relationships of Britain to her Colonies, Rules by which a Great Empire may be Reduced to a Small One
Educated: Born Boston, education sketchy
Notes: Scientist and politician; helped draft the American Constitution. Founded the influential social and debating society (The Junto Club)

20 Henry Fielding   1707–1754   British
Famous works: Tom Jones, The History of the Adventures of Joseph Andrews
Educated: Eton
Notes: Very sick much of his life with asthma and dropsy

21 Samuel Johnson   1709–1784   British
Famous works: Dictionary, The Vanity of Human Wishes
Educated: Pembroke College, Oxford
Notes: Famous lexicographer, critic and brilliant conversationalist and wit

22 Thomas Gray   1716–1771   British
Famous work: Elegy Written in a Country Churchyard
Educated: Eton and Peterhouse College, Cambridge
Notes: Letters are among finest in the language, incredible descriptive powers and wit

23 Oliver Goldsmith   1728–1774   Irish
Famous works: The Vicar of Wakefield, She Stoops to
Conquer, The Citizen of the World
Educated: Trinity College, Dublin
Notes: In his own words, he was mostly addicted to
gambling and was an experienced liar

24 Edmund Burke   1729–1797   Irish
Famous work: Reflections on the Revolution in France
Educated: Quakers School, Balitore, and Trinity College,
Dublin
Notes: Whig politician and political theorist. Founded
The Annual Register

25 William Cowper   1731–1800   British
Famous works: Table Talk, The Task
Educated: Westminster School, The Inner Temple (Law)
Notes: Trained as a lawyer and was converted to
evangelical Christianity

26 James Boswell   1740–1795   Scottish
Famous work: The Life of Dr Johnson
Educated: Edinburgh University (Law)
Notes: Felt thwarted because he did not attain the political
career he wanted

27 Fanny Burney   1752–1840   British
Famous works: Evelina, Cecilia, Camilla
Educated: Self-educated
Notes: Her diary is one of the best sources of first-hand
portraits of late eighteenth-century characters and life

28 George Crabbe   1754–1832   British
Famous work: The Village
Educated: Apprentice to a doctor
Notes: Narrative poet of grim humour

29 William Blake   1757–1827   British
Famous works: Songs of Innocence and Experience,
The Marriage of Heaven and Hell
Educated: Royal Academy at Somerset House
Notes: Volumes of meaning expressed in apparently simple
musical lines of his poetry

30 Robert Burns   1759–1796   Scottish
Famous works: Tam-o'Shanter, Auld Lang Syne
Educated: By his father and mother
Notes: Wrote most remarkable cantata, The Jolly Beggar

**31 William Cobbett
('Peter Porcupine')**   1762–1835   British
Famous works: Rural Rides, Cobbett's Political Register,
Porcupine's Gazette
Educated: Self-educated in army
Notes: His published output was enormous, from farming
to politics

32 William Wordsworth   1770–1850   British
Famous works: Daffodils, Sonnets, Ode on the Intimations
of Immortality, Prelude
Educated: Hawkshead Grammar School and St John's
College, Cambridge
Notes: Born in the English Lake District; a leading Romantic
poet

33 Sir Walter Scott   1771–1832   Scottish
Famous works: Ivanhoe, Kenilworth
Educated: Royal High School and University in Edinburgh
Notes: Wrote almost 40 novels from 1814 to 1832

34 Samuel Taylor Coleridge   1772–1834   British
Famous works: Rime of the Ancient Mariner, Kubla Khan
Educated: Jesus College, Cambridge
Notes: Romantic poet who collaborated on Lyrical Ballads
with William Wordsworth; addicted to opium

35 Jane Austen   1775–1817   British
Famous works: Emma, Mansfield Park, Pride and Prejudice
Educated: By her father
Notes: Portrayed middle-class society with remarkable
subtlety

36 Charles Lamb   1775–1834   British
Famous works: Essays of Elia, Tales from Shakespeare
(written with his sister Mary)
Educated: Christ's Hospital
Notes: Devoted his life to his sister, who was mentally
unstable

37 William Hazlitt   1778–1830   British
Famous works: The Characters of Shakespeare's Plays
Educated: Hackney College, London (Art and Metaphysics)
Notes: Ability as a critic with remarkable physical
description through his observant artistic eye

38 Thomas de Quincey   1785–1859   British
Famous works: Confessions of an Opium-eater
Educated: Manchester Grammar School
Notes: Addicted to opium; work of uneven quality

39 Lord George Gordon Byron   1788–1824   British
Famous works: Manfred, Don Juan, Childe Harold
Educated: Aberdeen Grammar School, Harrow School,
Trinity College, Cambridge
Notes: Enormously influential Romantic poet who became
involved in Italian and Greek revolutionary politics

40 James Fenimore Cooper   1789–1851   American
Famous works: The Spy, The Last of the Mohicans
Educated: Albany and Yale
Notes: A judge

41 Percy Bysshe Shelley   1792–1822   British
Famous works: Prometheus Unbound, Ode to the West Wind
Educated: University College, Oxford
Notes: Leading figure in the Romantic movement; drowned
in Italy at age of 30

42 John Clare   1793–1864   British
Famous works: The Shepherd's Calendar, Poems Descriptive
of Rural Life and Scenery
Educated: By his father
Notes: Known as the Peasant Poet; spent much of his life in
an asylum

43 John Keats   1795–1821   British
Famous works: Hyperion, Ode to Autumn
Educated: Harrow School and Enfield Academy
Notes: Romantic poet who was apprenticed to an apothecary
and qualified for study of surgery at Guy's Hospital. Died of
tuberculosis at 26

44 Thomas Carlyle   1795–1881   Scottish
Famous work: Sartor Resartus
Educated: Annan Grammar School, Edinburgh University
Notes: Lost the use of his right hand and could no longer write

45 Elizabeth Barrett Browning   1806–1861   British
Famous works: The Cry of the Children, Sonnets from the
Portuguese, Aurora Leigh
Educated: At home
Notes: Married Robert Browning. She was recommended as
Poet Laureate

46 Henry Wadsworth Longfellow   1807–1882   American
Famous works: Song of Hiawatha, The Courtship of Miles
Standish
Educated: Bowdoin, Portland, Maine
Notes: First poems published at 13

47 Edgar Allan Poe   1809–1849   American
Famous work: The Pit and the Pendulum
Educated: University of Virginia
Notes: Trained as a lawyer. Stories often weird and fantastic

48 Lord Alfred Tennyson   1809–1892   British
Famous works: Maud, In Memoriam, The Eagle
Educated: Louth Grammar School and Trinity College,
Cambridge
Notes: Poet Laureate

49 William Makepeace Thackeray   1811–1863   British
Famous works: Vanity Fair, The Virginians
Educated: Trinity College, Cambridge (Law)
Notes: Studied law before becoming a journalist and
novelist. Travelled in the US and died at 52 of heartstrain

50 Charles Dickens   1812–1870   British
Famous works: Pickwick Papers, Oliver Twist, etc.
Educated: Intermittently
Notes: Novelist known for his memorable
characters and exposure of Victorian
social evils.

51 Robert Browning   1812–1889   British
Famous works: The Pied Piper of Hamelin, Home Thoughts
from Abroad
Educated: Mostly at home
Notes: Great romance of literary history with Elizabeth Barrett

52 Anthony Trollope   1815–1882   British
Famous works: The Barchester Chronicles,
The Way We Live Now
Educated: Harrow School
Notes: Clerk in the Post Office

53 Charlotte Brontë   1816–1855   British
Famous work: Jane Eyre
Educated: At a very harsh boarding school later portrayed
as Lowood in Jane Eyre
Notes: Taught in Brussels

54 Emily Brontë   1818–1848   British
Famous work: Wuthering Heights
Educated: At home in Haworth
Notes: Died of tuberculosis

55 Charles Kingsley   1819–1875   British
Famous works: The Water-Babies, Westward Ho!
Educated: King's College, London, and Magdalene College,
Cambridge
Notes: Deeply concerned with social reform but opposed
to change brought about by force

56 George Eliot (Mary Ann Evans)   1819–1880   British
Famous works: Silas Marner, Middlemarch
Educated: Privately at Coventry
Notes: Read extensively in theology and languages.
Left school following death of mother

57 Walt Whitman   1819–1892   American
Famous work: Leaves of Grass
Educated: Brooklyn
Notes: Led a wandering life and did hospital work during
the American Civil War

58 John Ruskin   1819–1900   British
Famous work: Modern Painters
Educated: By parents and at Christchurch, Oxford
Notes: Art critic and social reformer who laid the
foundations of the Arts and Crafts movement

59 Anne Brontë   1820–1849   British
Famous work: Agnes Grey
Educated: At home in Haworth
Notes: Used pseudonym Acton Bell. Died of tuberculosis at age 29

60 Matthew Arnold   1822–1888   British
Famous work: Dover Beach
Educated: Rugby School and Balliol College, Oxford
Notes: Poet and critic

61 Emily Dickinson   1830–1886   American
Famous work: The Chariot
Educated: Amherst School and Academy, then Mount Holyoke Female Seminary
Notes: America's greatest woman poet, who always wrote in secret. Over 2000 poems discovered after her death

62 Lewis Carroll
(Charles Lutwidge Dodgson)   1832–1898   British
Famous works: Alice Through the Looking Glass, Alice in Wonderland
Educated: Rugby School and Oxford (Maths)
Notes: A lecturer in mathematics at Oxford

63 Mark Twain
(Samuel Langhorn Clemens)   1835–1910   American
Famous works: Tom Sawyer, Huckleberry Finn
Educated: Left school at 12
Notes: Printer's apprentice and river pilot who became leading American humourist

64 Algernon Charles Swinburne   1837–1909   British
Famous works: Atalanta in Calydon, Aeschylus and Sappho
Educated: Eton College and Balliol College, Oxford
Notes: His poetry often shocked with its eroticism

65 Thomas Hardy   1840–1928   British
Famous works: Far From the Madding Crowd, Tess of the D'Urbervilles
Educated: Local schools in Dorset
Notes: Apprenticed to an architect, he became a novelist and poet

66 Henry James   1843–1916   American
Famous works: The Turn of the Screw, The Wings of the Dove
Educated: Private tutors and part Law School
Notes: Europhile; prolific writings explored the Anglo-American gulf. Dense narrative sometimes difficult for readers to understand

67 Gerard Manley Hopkins   1844–1889   British
Famous work: The Wreck of the Deutschland
Educated: Balliol College, Oxford
Notes: Was an ordained priest and professor of Greek at University of Dublin. Felt conflict between poetry and religious calling. Died of typhoid

68 Oscar Wilde   1854–1900   Irish
Famous works: The Importance of Being Earnest, The Picture of Dorian Gray
Educated: Portora Royal School and Trinity College, Dublin, and Magdalen College, Oxford
Notes: Famous for wit and epigrammatic brilliance. Leader of the cult of 'Art for Art's sake'; imprisoned for homosexuality

69 George Bernard Shaw   1856–1950   Irish
Famous works: Man and Superman, Pygmalion
Educated: Left day school at 15
Notes: Became known as a journalist and critic and wrote nearly 60 plays. Letters edited by D H. Lawrence

70 Joseph Conrad   1857–1924   British
Famous works: Lord Jim, The Secret Agent, Under Western Eyes, Nostromo
Educated: Cracow, Poland
Notes: Born Polish Ukraine but exiled. Became a Master Mariner in British Merchant Navy. Wrote with clarity but never learnt to speak English well

71 Sir Arthur Conan Doyle   1859–1930   British
Famous works: Sherlock Holmes series
Educated: Edinburgh University (medicine)
Notes: A doctor who wrote short stories to supplement his income. Creator of the fictional character Sherlock Holmes. Worked as a senior physician in South Africa during the Boer War. Knighted in 1902

72 J(ames) M(atthew) Barrie   1860–1937   Scottish
Famous work: Peter Pan
Educated: By his mother, Dumfries Academy and Edinburgh University
Notes: The Boy David, his final play, awaits revival so that it can be properly judged on the stage

73 W(illiam) B(utler) Yeats   1865–1939   Irish
Famous works: Adoration of the Magi, The Wild Swans at Coole
Educated: London, Art School
Notes: Encouraged by his father, his Celtic inheritance was a powerful influence for him. Founded Dublin Hermetic Society to promote the study of Oriental religions and theosophy. Fell in love with Maude Gonne but she refused to marry him. He married a medium, Georgie Hyde-Lees, and they attempted 'automatic writing' with striking results

74 Rudyard Kipling   1865–1936   British
Famous works: Jungle Book, Just So Stories
Educated: United Services College, Devon
Notes: Born in Bombay, but left by family in London. Nobel Prize-winner in 1907

75 H.G. (Herbert George) Wells   1866–1946   British
Famous works: The Time Machine, Island of Dr Moreau, Wheels of Chance, Love and Mr Lewisham, Kipps
Educated: Royal College of Science, Kensington
Notes: Mixed scientific journalism with teaching. Wrote science fiction and fantasy stories side-by-side. Predicted many inventions that have come to pass

76 John Galsworthy   1867–1933   British
Famous works: The Forsyte Saga, The Silver Spoon, The Modern Comedy
Educated: Harrow School and New College, Oxford (Law)
Notes: Used pseudonym of John Sinjohn until after his fifth book. Wrote 31 full-length plays

77 Arnold Bennett   1867–1931   British
Famous works: The Old Wives' Tale, Clayhanger, Anna of the Five Towns, Riceyman Steps
Educated: Burslem Endowed School

Notes: Went to work for his father, a solicitor, at 18. Became a prolific journalist and novelist, setting much of his fiction in the Potteries district of Staffordshire

78 Walter de la Mare   1873–1956   British
Famous works: The Listeners
Educated: St Paul's Choir School
Notes: A poet, storyteller and novelist, whose work is characterised by an atmosphere of mystery. Wrote unpatronisingly for children, and continued to write into his eighties. Sometimes wrote under the name of Walter Ramal

79 G(ilbert) K(eith) Chesterton   1874–1936   British
Famous works: The Innocence of Father Brown, The Flying Inn
Educated: St Paul's School, Slade School of Art
Notes: Studied art, became a journalist and entered the Catholic Church in 1922

80 William Somerset Maugham   1874–1965   British
Famous works: Liza of Lambeth, Of Human Bondage
Educated: King's School, Canterbury and St Thomas' Hospital (Medicine)
Notes: Storyteller of genius with a sardonic view of human behaviour; anti-romantic and mercilessly observant, with an unrivalled skill in realising the climax of a story

81 John Masefield   1878–1967   British
Famous works: Salt-water Ballads, Reynard the Fox
Educated: King's School, Warwickshire
Notes: Went to sea but ill-health made him decide to become a writer

82 E(dward) M(organ) Forster   1879–1970   British
Famous works: The Longest Journey, A Room with a View, Where Angels Fear to Tread, Passage to India
Educated: Tonbridge School, King's College, Cambridge
Notes: Enjoyed exploring the contrast between 'buttoned-up' British culture and the warmer, more passionate cultures of other countries. Member of the Apostle Society, Chicago

83 James Joyce   1882–1969   Irish
Famous works: Ulysses, Finnegans Wake, Portrait of the Artist as a Young Man
Educated: Jesuit School, Kildare, University College, Dublin
Notes: Ulysses published in serial form but was stopped as obscene material

84 D(avid) H(erbert) Lawrence   1885–1930   British
Famous works: Sons and Lovers, Lady Chatterley's Lover
Educated: Nottingham High School
Notes: Tried to explore emotion and sexuality on a deep level. Disharmony of home and parents strongly affected him

85 Ezra Pound   1885–1972   American
Famous work: The Spirit of Romance
Educated: University of Pennsylvania and Hamilton College, New York
Notes: Travelled to Europe where he met writers, such as T.S. Eliot, W.B. Yeats and Ernest Hemingway. His anti-Semitism and sympathy with Mussolini led to his arrest and subsequent confinement in an asylum until 1958

86 Olaf Stapledon   1886–1950   British
Famous works: Star Maker, Last and First Men, Last Men in London, Sirius, A Man Divided
Educated: Abbotsholme School; Balliol College, Oxford; Liverpool University
Notes: Father of modern science fiction and a freedom fighter. University Lecturer in English Literature, Psychology, Philosophy and Industrial History

87 Edith Sitwell   1887–1964   British
Famous works: Façade (set to music by William Walton), Gold Coast Customs
Educated: At home
Notes: One of the most celebrated of English women, awarded four honorary doctorates. 1948 Nobel Prize-winner

88 Joyce Cary   1888–1957   British
Famous works: Mister Johnson, The Horse's Mouth
Educated: Tonbridge Wells, Clifton College, Trinity College, Oxford
Notes: Worked with the British Red Cross in the Balkan Wars and as a District Magistrate in Nigeria. Wrote his first novel at 44

89 T(homas) S(tearns) Eliot   1888–1965   British
Famous works: The Waste Land, The Four Quartets,
Old Possum's Book of Practical Cats (on which the musical
Cats was based)
Educated: Harvard University and Merton College, Oxford
Notes: The term 'Old Possum' was Ezra Pound's nickname for
Eliot and referred to his soft-footed, circuitous approach. Born
in St Louis, Missouri, he became a British subject in 1927

90 Ivy Compton-Burnett   1892–1969   British
Famous work: Pastors and Masters
Educated: Royal Holloway College, University of London
Notes: Her books deal with family relationships objectively
and unsentimentally

91 J(ohn) B(oynton) Priestley   1894–1984   British
Famous works: The Good Companions, Dangerous Corner
Educated: Trinity College, Cambridge
Notes: Wrote essays, literary criticism, travel, fiction,
autobiography and over 40 plays

92 F(rancis) Scott Fitzgerald   1896–1940   American
Famous works: Tender Is the Night, The Great Gatsby
Educated: Newman School, New Jersey, and Princeton
Notes: Led a life that epitomised the self-indulgence of the
'jazz age'. His glamorous wife Zelda suffered from mental
illness and he became a chronic alcoholic

93 William Harrison Faulkner   1897–1962   American
Famous works: The Sound and the Fury, As I Lay Dying
Educated: University of Mississippi
Notes: Won Pulitzer and Nobel Prizes. His novels provide
insight to a grim and complex era of American life

94 Ernest Hemingway   1898–1961   American
Famous works: A Farewell to Arms, For Whom the Bell
Tolls, The Old Man and the Sea
Educated: Oak Park School, Illinois
Notes: Known for 'masculine' writing style. 1954 Nobel
Prize-winner. Committed suicide

95 Noël Coward   1899–1973   British
Famous works: Private Lives, Blithe Spirit, Brief Encounter
Educated: Italia Conti Stage School
Notes: Successful actor and playwright. Flawless ear for spoken dialogue

96 George Orwell   1903–1950   British
Famous works: Animal Farm, 1984
Educated: Eton College
Notes: Served with Indian Civil Police in Burma, then returned to Europe as a teacher. Vivid commentator on reality of deprivation and became increasingly pessimistic about affairs at home and abroad

97 Evelyn Waugh   1903–1966   British
Famous works: Vile Bodies, Brideshead Revisited
Educated: Lancing School and Hertford College, Oxford
Notes: Worked as a teacher and a journalist

98 C(ecil) Day Lewis   1904–1972   British
Famous works: From Feathers to Iron, Overtures to Death
Educated: Sherborne School, Wadham College, Oxford
Notes: Poet Laureate and critic. Under pseudonym Nicholas Blake wrote 20 detective novels

99 Graham Greene   1904–1991   British
Famous works: The Heart of the Matter, Brighton Rock
Educated: Berkhamsted School, Balliol College, Oxford
Notes: Novelist, journalist and playwright. Awarded British Order of Merit in 1986

100 Samuel Beckett   1906–1987   Anglo-Irish
Famous works: Waiting for Godot, Malone Dies, Endgame
Educated: Trinity College, Dublin
Notes: Strongly associated with Theatre of the Absurd. Writings characterised by black humour and bleak interior monologues

Top 20 Geniuses
of All Time

Genius is often thought to be a rare gift – something indefinable,

something mysterious, and something that occurs only once in a lifetime.

In reality, genius is something quite different.

Genius is a range of mental qualities that can be measured and, more importantly, nurtured and grown (as you are doing with your own mental abilities in this book).

The standard qualities of genius include: Vision; Desire; Faith; Commitment; Planning; Persistence; Learning from mistakes; Subject knowledge; Mental Literacy; Imagination; Positive attitude; Auto-suggestion; Intuition; Real Master-Mind Group (Group of closest friends and advisors); Internal Master-Mind Group (Heroes, heroines and role models); Truth/honesty; Facing fears/courage; Creativity/flexibility; Love of the task; and Energy – Physical/sensual.

It will be useful to check your own development in these areas. Where you are strong you can continue to grow those strengths; where you are weak you can use your strengths to help make you stronger. Rank yourself out of 100 (0 = non-existent, 100 = perfect). Try to be as honest as possible, and retest yourself every few months.

In those geniuses who are defined as great by history, virtually all these qualities were developed to the maximum. How, then, can you discriminate between them? How can you assess the qualities of genius-within-genius?

Once again, there are measurable categories: dominance in the field of activity; active longevity; polymathy (skill and knowledge in many disciplines, as you are developing in *Master Your Memory*) and versatility; strength and energy; intelligence quotient; on-going influence on the development of the human race; prolificness; and achievement of prime goal. Add to these universality of vision, breakthrough originality; and a deliberate desire to pass on their new knowledge through teaching or academies, and a ranking becomes eminently possible. Tony Buzan, Grandmaster Raymond Keene, OBE, and a committee of international leaders in the fields of education, science, art, sport and Mind Sports, after years of impassioned discussion, settled on the rankings below. It may be interesting for you to devise your own list before memorising this one – see what areas you agree with the compilers! (For more information on genius see *Buzan's Book of Genius*.)

TOP 20 GENIUSES

		Born	Died	Nationality	Area
1	Leonardo da Vinci	1452	1519	Italian	Artist/Inventor
2	William Shakespeare	1564	1616	British	Writer
3	Great Pyramid Builders	c. 2550 BC		Egyptians	Architects
4	Johann Wolfgang von Goethe	1749	1832	German	Writer
5	Michelangelo	1475	1564	Italian	Artist
6	Sir Isaac Newton	1642	1727	British	Inventor
7	Thomas Jefferson	1743	1826	American	Politician
8	Alexander the Great	356 BC	323 BC	Macedonian	Monarch
9	Phidias	500 BC	432 BC	Greek	Artist
10	Albert Einstein	1879	1955	German	Scientist
11	Thomas Alva Edison	1847	1931	American	Inventor
12	Homer	Eighth century BC		Greek	Writer
13	Plato	428 BC	348 BC	Greek	Philosopher
14	Euclid	c. 300 BC		Greek	Teacher
15	Elizabeth I	1533	1603	British	Monarch
16	Archimedes	287 BC	212 BC	Greek	Scientist
17	Aristotle	384 BC	322 BC	Greek	Philosopher
18	Filippo Brunelleschi	1377	1446	Italian	Artist
19	Andrew Carnegie	1835	1918	Scottish	Industrialist
20	First Ch'in Emperor	259 BC	210 BC	Chinese	Monarch

Shakespeare
The Complete Plays

 **Preview**

- The Greek Plays
- The Roman Plays
- English Historical Plays
- The Tragedies
- The Comedies
- The Moral Plays
- The Last Plays

The plays of William Shakespeare are regarded by many as the most comprehensive and masterful literary works in the English language, if not all languages. From them come an enormous number of the expressions and concepts we use today, and the names of many of the characters have become a major part of our cultural heritage.

Once you have a grasp of the basic plot and characters of Shakespeare's plays, you will be able to understand many other literary works more readily, to grasp more rapidly points being made in conversations, and to refer yourself, with sure knowledge, to Shakespearean events and characters. In addition to this, you will easily be able to unravel the 'who was related to whom, in what play, when and where?' conundrums with which so many people find themselves being faced. Rather than subsequently 'giving up' on Shakespeare because he is 'too confusing', you will be like a literary Sherlock Holmes, already hot on the trail of your informational goals.

One excellent method for using SEM^3 in conjunction with Shakespeare is to set aside an appropriate section of SEM^3

specifically for Shakespeare, and to memorise the basic plot and character for each play when you are about to see or hear it performed. We have set out the plays in such a way that there is a memorable quotation and chief characters to memorise as well as a summary of the plot. In this way, what you are memorising will be immediately relevant, will assist you with an understanding of the play by which you are about to be entertained, and will enable the play to assist you in the memorisation of itself! On the reverse side of this coin, you will find that using SEM^3 to help you memorise Shakespeare will encourage you to re-investigate the Bard, thus enhancing your social and cultural life.

Here is a list of the plays, in order of composition:

1589–92	1. *Henry VI*, 2. *Henry VI*, 3. *Henry VI*
1592–93	4. *Richard III*, 5. *The Comedy of Errors*
1593–94	6. *Titus Andronicus*, 7. *The Taming of the Shrew*
1594–95	8. *The Two Gentlemen of Verona*, 9. *Love's Labour's Lost*, 10. *Romeo and Juliet*
1595–96	11. *Richard II*, 12. *A Midsummer Night's Dream*
1596–97	13. *King John*, 14. *The Merchant of Venice*
1597–98	15. *Henry IV*, 16. *Henry IV*
1598–99	17. *Much Ado About Nothing*, 18. *Henry V*
1599–1600	19. *Julius Caesar*, 20. *As You Like It*
1600–01	21. *Hamlet*, 22. *The Merry Wives of Windsor*
1601–02	23. *Twelfth Night*, 24. *Troilus and Cressida*
1602–03	25. *All's Well That Ends Well*
1604–05	26. *Measure For Measure*, 27. *Othello*
1605–06	28. *King Lear*, 29. *Macbeth*
1606–07	30. *Antony and Cleopatra*
1607–08	31. *Coriolanus*, 32. *Timon of Athens*
1608–09	33. *Pericles*
1609–10	34. *Cymbeline*
1610–11	35. *The Winter's Tale*
1611–12	36. *The Tempest*
1612–13	37. *Henry VIII**

The plays have been categorised in a new way to help with the understanding and memorisation of them. The Greek Plays, The Roman Plays, English Historical Plays, The Tragedies, The Comedies, The Moral Plays and The Last Plays.

---

* *The Tempest* is widely regarded as Shakespeare's final play. Although *Henry VIII* was completed later, it is thought to have been in collaboration with Fletcher and Beaumont.

The Greek Plays

Unlike the Roman plays, Shakespeare's Greek plays do not fit any historical theme. They are essentially isolated stories taken from the Greek classical world. Of particular note is *Troilus and Cressida*, in which Shakespeare turns his hand to one of the most famous legends of all time, Homer's *Siege of Troy*.

1 ● Pericles
Prince of Tyre

Quote: *'Oh you gods! Why do you make us love your goodly gifts and snatch them straight away?'*

Dramatis Personae

1 PERICLES, Prince of Tyre
2 CERIMON, a lord of Ephesus
3 MARINA, daughter to Pericles and Thaisa

This play is based upon the ancient tale of Apollonius of Tyre, a Greek romance. Pericles, who is a prince, loses his daughter and sets off on a long journey to regain her. He has many adventures, twice being shipwrecked. Eventually, with the help of Cerimon, a lord of Ephesus and also a physician, he finds her. The play may be summarised as: father has daughter; father loses daughter; father searches for daughter; father regains daughter.

2 ● Timon of Athens

Quote: *'Men shut their doors against a setting sun.'*

Dramatis Personae

1 TIMON of Athens

Timon of Athens is a biting satire on human ingratitude and disloyalty. The play starts with Timon as a wealthy man, a generous host and one who gives lavishly to his friends. Suddenly creditors demand repayment and he is bankrupt.

Timon sees this as a perfect opportunity for his friends to prove their brotherhood and justify his belief in the goodness of man. However, each friend turns him down, a shocking and cynical betrayal of Timon's trust in human nature. He becomes a disillusioned misanthropic hermit and dies in a tomb by the sea.

3 ● Troilus and Cressida

Quote: *'Take but degree away, untune that string
and hark! what discord follows.'*

Dramatis Personae

1 HECTOR
2 TROILUS
3 PANDARUS, uncle to Cressida
4 AGAMEMNON, the Grecian general
5 ACHILLES
6 ULYSSES, Grecian commander
7 THERSITES, a deformed and scurrilous Grecian
8 CRESSIDA, daughter to Calchas
9 CALCHAS, father of Cressida and a Trojan priest
10 PARIS

Troilus and Cressida is Shakespeare's theatrical interpretation of
Homer's epic poem *The Iliad*. It recounts the siege of Troy, and the
refusal of the great hero Achilles to join in the siege because he has
been insulted by the Greek leader Agamemnon. The play chronicles
internal power struggles, the eventual return of Achilles to the war,
and his revenge against Hector, the hero of Troy. Against the
background of the ten-year war is set the story of Troilus and his
faithless lover Cressida. The play ends with the fall of Troy.

The Roman Plays

Shakespeare's Roman plays span the entire pageant of Roman
history. *Coriolanus* details an epic moment from the Roman
Republic; *Julius Caesar* and *Antony and Cleopatra* depict the birth
pangs of the Roman Empire; while *Titus Andronicus* is set during
the Empire's decline and shows the accompanying collapse of
morals and political structures as the Empire loses its traditions
and direction under pressure from the Barbarians.

1 ● Coriolanus

Quote: *'His nature is too noble for the world.'*

Dramatis Personae

1 CAIUS MARCIUS, afterwards CAIUS MARCIUS
   CORIOLANUS
2 TULLUS AUFIDIUS, general of the Volscians
3 VOLUMNIA, mother to Coriolanus
4 VIRGILIA, wife to Coriolanus

The story is a legend from the early days of the foundation of Rome's greatness. The general Coriolanus defeats Rome's chief enemy, the Volsces. He returns victorious to Rome expecting and expected to be made political as well as military leader. His arrogance, however, causes both the leaders and the population to rise against him. In revenge he joins the Volsces as their leader and vows to wreak havoc on Rome. At the last moment Volumnia and Virgilia, mother and wife of Coriolanus, persuade him not to attack Rome. As a result, the Volsces, considering him a traitor, assassinate Coriolanus.

2 ● Julius Caesar

Quote: *'Friends, Romans, Countrymen, lend me your ears.'*

Dramatis Personae

1 JULIUS CAESAR, later as a GHOST
2 OCTAVIUS CAESAR
3 MARCUS ANTONIUS
4 MARCUS BRUTUS
5 CASSIUS
6 A SOOTHSAYER

Julius Caesar describes the early greatness and the assassination of the Roman dictator Caesar and sets the scene for an analysis of the foundation of the Roman Empire. The play recounts how Cassius and other conspirators plot to assassinate Julius Caesar and to make Brutus their leader. They stab Caesar to death on the Ides of March, as had been prophesied. Antony is given permission to speak at Caesar's funeral and, in a famous speech, rouses the crowds to fury at what has happened. The conspirators Cassius and Brutus raise armies, are defeated in battle and commit suicide.

3 ● Antony and Cleopatra

Quote: *'Age cannot wither her, nor custom stale
her infinite variety.'*

Dramatis Personae

1 MARK ANTONY
2 OCTAVIUS CAESAR
3 DOMITIUS ENOBARBUS
4 CLEOPATRA, Queen of Egypt
5 M. AEMILIUS LEPIDUS
6 OCTAVIA, sister to Caesar and wife to Antony

Antony and Cleopatra is the sequel to *Julius Caesar.* It tells how one of Caesar's chief lieutenants, Mark Antony, travels to Egypt to take over the eastern half of the Roman dominions. There he falls in love with Cleopatra, is obliged to return home, agrees to marry Octavia, Caesar's sister, but returns to Cleopatra in Egypt. Antony attempts to use Egypt as a base from which to take over the entire ancient Roman Empire. He is challenged by Octavius, Julius Caesar's nephew, who defeats him and rises to become the first Emperor Augustus. Having been defeated and hearing a false report that Cleopatra is dead, Antony commits suicide. Hearing of his death, Cleopatra similarly commits suicide, and the 'immortal' couple are buried together.

4 ◦ Titus Andronicus

Quote: *'She is a woman, therefore may be wooed. She is a woman, therefore may be won.'*

Dramatis Personae

1 SATURNINUS, oldest son to the late Emperor of Rome, and afterwards declared EMPEROR
2 TITUS ANDRONICUS, a noble Roman, general against the Goths
3 TAMORA, Queen of the Goths
4 LAVINIA, daughter to Titus Andronicus

This play is academic, ambitious and masterfully planned, with a multiplicity of fearful events and climaxes. It begins in the late fourth century AD, during the gradual decline of the Roman Empire, when it is besieged by Goths. The great Roman general Titus kills the Gothic king, and continues the battle against the king's sons, but is gradually supplanted at Court by scheming rival factions. The play shows how he wreaks terrible revenge, including baking the sons of his enemies into a pie! Revenge complete, Titus commits suicide.

English Historical Plays

Shakespeare's historical plays, apart from including some superb characters such as Sir John Falstaff and Prince Hal, detail a crucial period in English history, starting with the dethronement of King Richard II, covering Henry V's invasion of France in the Wars of the Roses, and culminating in the establishment of the Tudor dynasty. Queen Elizabeth I, one of Shakespeare's main patrons, was of course one of the main Tudor monarchs. The plays commence with the depiction of England in turmoil, pass through the brief military glory of Henry V, see the country plunged once again into chaos during the Wars of the Roses, and finally show order being triumphantly restored as the Tudor King Henry VII ascends the throne. The historical period covered is essentially 100 years, from 1385 to 1485. The sole exception in the historical pageant is the play *King John* which is separate from the sequence and rarely performed.

1 • The Life and Death of King John
Quote: *'Come the three corners of the world in arms,*
and we shall shock them.'

Dramatis Personae
1 KING JOHN
2 PRINCE HENRY, son to the King
3 ARTHUR, Duke of Bretagne, nephew to the King
4 HUBERT DE BURGH
5 PHILIP THE BASTARD, his half-brother, later dubbed Richard Plantagenet
6 CARDINAL PANDULPH, the Pope's legate

This play explores the motives and behaviour of men competing for power. Events are concentrated around the fate of Arthur, and the foreshortening of the time scheme results in a dramatic intensification of the pressures in the conflict. John's corrupt greed for power is set against the ruthless fanaticism of Pandulph. Meanwhile Hubert and the Bastard move from cynicism and detachment to self-possession and integrity.

At the beginning of the play, John is seen as a fallible, uncertain, imperfect monarch, successful at first, and with his moment of glory in the full Protestant tradition as he confronts Pandulph. He is, however, increasingly subject to the corrupting power of political need, so that his final collapse is total.

2 • The Tragedy of King Richard II
Quote: *'This happy breed of men, this little world, this precious stone*
set in a silver sea . . . This England.'

Dramatis Personae
1 KING RICHARD II
2 JOHN OF GAUNT, DUKE OF LANCASTER
3 HENRY, surnamed BOLINGBROKE, DUKE OF HEREFORD, son to John of Gaunt; afterwards KING HENRY IV

4 EARL OF NORTHUMBERLAND
5 SIR PIERCE OF EXTON

Richard II is a weak king who has failed to maintain England's military supremacy over her old enemy, France. Among Richard's unwise acts are the levying of various illegal taxes, and the confiscation of the property of John of Gaunt (Bolingbroke's father) on his death. As a consequence, Bolingbroke eventually overthrows Richard, who is sent to Pontefract, where he is murdered by Exton, who presents the body to Bolingbroke. He in turn feels remorse and goes on a crusade to atone for Richard's death. Bolingbroke eventually becomes King Henry IV.

3 • The First Part of King Henry IV
Quote: *'What is honour? A Word – what is that word . . . Air.'*

Dramatis Personae
1 KING HENRY THE FOURTH
2 HENRY, PRINCE OF WALES
3 HENRY PERCY, EARL OF NORTHUMBERLAND
4 HENRY PERCY, surnamed HOTSPUR, his son
5 SIR JOHN FALSTAFF
6 MISTRESS QUICKLY, hostess of a tavern in Eastcheap
7 THOMAS PERCY, EARL OF WORCESTER

Henry Bolingbroke, now the king, has trouble with his son Henry, Prince of Wales (Hal), who spends too much time in the tavern drinking with the 'low-life' Falstaff and getting involved in petty crime. Henry also has trouble with the Earl of Worcester, the Earl of Northumberland and his son, Hotspur, who plan a rebellion, culminating in the Battle of Shrewsbury. In the battle Prince Hal kills Hotspur, the plot being complicated by Falstaff who claims that it was he who did so. The play ends as King Henry prepares for the next battle, against still more conspirators.

4 • The Second Part of King Henry IV
Quote: *'I am not only witty in myself, but the cause that wit is in other men.'*

Dramatis Personae
1 KING HENRY IV
2 HENRY, PRINCE OF WALES afterwards KING HENRY V
3 LORD CHIEF JUSTICE of the King's Bench

4 SIR JOHN FALSTAFF
5 SHALLOW ⎱ country justices
6 SILENCE ⎰
7 PRINCE JOHN OF LANCASTER
8 EARL OF NORTHUMBERLAND
9 SCROOP, ARCHBISHOP OF YORK

Rebellions continue, this time from the Archbishop of York and the Earl of Northumberland. The Archbishop is defeated by Prince John of Lancaster and the Earl of Northumberland is defeated by the Sheriff of Yorkshire.

After all the major rebellions have been put down, Henry eventually dies. Before he does he is reconciled with his son Hal, who develops from a riotous young prince into a just and wise ruler. His old friend Falstaff, now a knight, still gets into mischief but is no longer suitable company for the new King, who sends him to prison, but promises him a small pension.

5 ● The Life of King Henry V

Quote: *'Once more unto the breach dear friends, once more.'*

Dramatis Personae

1 KING HENRY V
2 PISTOL
3 LEWIS, THE DAUPHIN
4 KATHERINE, daughter to Charles and Isabel
5 DUKE OF BEDFORD, brother to the King
6 EARL OF SALISBURY
7 ARCHBISHOP OF CANTERBURY

The Archbishop of Canterbury advises the King that his descent from Isabella, the French Queen of Edward II, gives him the right to the French throne, and the Church would subsidise his going to war with France. Henry realises that this will also help to quell the internal disquiet from his own barons who are restless partly because Henry's own family is a usurper line.

The Dauphin mockingly sends Henry a box of tennis-balls in response to his claims to certain French dukedoms, so Henry promises war. The English take Harfleur but the army is weakened by disease and the French are much stronger. Henry encourages his soldiers and, against all odds, the French are defeated, and Henry takes the French throne. Henry develops into the model of a military monarch, and after the defeat of the French unites the Royal Houses by marrying Katherine, daughter of the French King.

6 ● The First Part of King Henry VI

Quote: *'From off this brier pluck a white rose with me.'*
'Pluck a red rose from off this thorn with me.'

Dramatis Personae

1 KING HENRY VI
2 DUKE OF GLOUCESTER, uncle to the King and Lord Protector
3 HENRY BEAUFORT, BISHOP OF WINCHESTER, great-uncle to the King, afterwards CARDINAL
4 DUKE OF BEDFORD, uncle to the King and Regent of France
5 RICHARD PLANTAGENET, son of Richard late Earl of Cambridge, afterwards DUKE OF YORK
6 EARL OF SALISBURY
7 LORD TALBOT, afterwards Earl of Shrewsbury
8 CHARLES, Dauphin, and afterwards King, of France
9 DUKE OF BURGUNDY
10 MARGARET, daughter of Reignier, afterwards married to King Henry
11 JOAN LA PUCELLE, commonly called Joan of Arc

Henry V has died young, and his infant son Henry VI is technically on the throne. However, rival factions of barons now contend for mastery and the realm begins to weaken. The play deals with the multiple conflicts between the English and French. On the French side, Joan of Arc uses her persuasive powers to provoke the Duke of Burgundy's defection from the English cause.

The play ends with the seizure of Margaret of Anjou and Henry's betrothal to her, and with the Duke of York's capture of Joan and her trial and execution.

7 ● The Second Part of King Henry VI

Quote: *'Let's kill all the lawyers.'*

Dramatis Personae

1 KING HENRY VI
2 HUMPHREY, DUKE OF GLOUCESTER, his uncle
3 CARDINAL BEAUFORT, BISHOP OF WINCHESTER, great-uncle to the King
4 JACK CADE, a rebel

The young Henry is now truly king, but the focus of the barons is on the quest for control. They fight among themselves, rather than defeating the ancient enemy France. The play shows a nation's abandonment of its vision and its social order. In this play Henry is defied by his wife, nobles and people; the rule of law breaks down; justice becomes a victim of whim and ambition; goodness is scorned in families and in the nation; and Christian virtue appears impotent when opposed by vigorous self-interest and violence.

The conditions necessary for correct rule are represented by King Henry and the Duke of Gloucester, Protector of the Realm. The play revolves around the reaction to the positive virtues of these two men. The Crown begins to totter.

8 ● The Third Part of King Henry VI

Quote: *'Proud setter up and puller down of kings.'*

Dramatis Personae

1 KING HENRY VI
2 RICHARD PLANTAGENET, DUKE OF YORK
3 EDWARD, Earl of March, afterwards KING EDWARD IV
4 GEORGE, afterwards DUKE OF CLARENCE
5 RICHARD, afterwards DUKE OF GLOUCESTER
6 EARL OF WARWICK
7 QUEEN MARGARET

This play takes place during the 20-year period from 1455 to 1475, the time of the Wars of the Roses. The play focuses on the Duke of York, and his sons Edward, George and Richard, who plan to seize the throne from Henry VI of the House of Lancaster. England, still torn by internal strife and moral decay, is weakening; France is lost; and the Duke of York is killed in battle, although the House of York eventually triumphs. Henry VI is assassinated and the Duke of York's son Edward becomes king.

9 ● The Tragedy of King Richard III

Quote: *'A horse, a horse, my kingdom for a horse.'*

Dramatis Personae

1 KING EDWARD IV
2 RICHARD, DUKE OF GLOUCESTER,
   afterwards KING RICHARD III

3 HENRY, EARL OF RICHMOND,
   afterwards KING HENRY VII
4 DUKE OF BUCKINGHAM, later as a GHOST

With Edward IV now king, Richard, Duke of Gloucester, the Duke of York's youngest son, plots to seize the throne. His problem lies in the fact that he is fifth in the line of succession.

The play follows his machiavellian practices as he assassinates every single possible rival claimant, including, in a famous scene, the two young princes. He eventually becomes king and plans to marry Edward's daughter Elizabeth.

At the end of the play, having become king, his evil deeds catch up with him. The ghosts of all Richard's victims appear and prophesy his death. He is overthrown by Henry, Earl of Richmond, at the Battle of Bosworth. Henry becomes King Henry VII and unites the Houses of York and Lancaster, the groups of previously contending barons. Peace reigns.

10 ● The Famous History of the Life of King Henry VIII

Quote: *'In her days everyman shall eat in safety under his own vine . . . and sing the merry songs of peace to all his neighbours.'*

Dramatis Personae

1 KING HENRY VIII
2 CARDINAL WOLSEY
3 DUKE OF BUCKINGHAM
4 QUEEN KATHARINE, wife to King Henry,
   afterwards divorced
5 ANNE BULLEN, her Maid of Honour, afterwards Queen

This is Shakespeare's only play to be entitled a 'Famous History' and takes unusual care to be historically accurate. The play's form is wave-like, with great swells of events bearing the King and leading figures upward and downward, to and from high places.

The Duke of Buckingham, having decided to challenge the overbearing Wolsey, is arrested before he can take measures either of attack or defence. Queen Katharine demonstrates her courage by speaking for him and against Cardinal Wolsey; Buckingham is executed. Meanwhile the King starts to raise Anne Boleyn (Bullen) to the throne, as Katharine falls from grace and there is a divorce trial. Then even Wolsey is convicted of exorbitant gains and falls from power. To counter-balance this, Anne is crowned and

Princess Elizabeth is born. *Henry VIII* finishes in a triumphant mood and is clearly meant to celebrate the reign.

By this time Henry and Anne Boleyn have produced a daughter who eventually becomes Queen Elizabeth. The play is essentially a hymn of praise to the Tudor dynasty and to Queen Elizabeth who was, of course, on the throne while Shakespeare was writing this play.

The Tragedies

In his tragedies Shakespeare adopts the classical Greek definition of tragedy put forward by Aristotle in his *Poetics* – they all show a great man brought to a tragic end through the ineluctable workings of a fatal flaw. The flaw, in some circumstances, could be considered a strength, but as the plays develop it always turns out to be an Achilles' heel. For example, Macbeth's ambition is a great driving force in his career, but, taken to excess, it leads to his downfall. With Lear, the tragic flaw is pride; in Othello, it is jealousy (though it was Othello's enormous possessiveness towards Desdemona that led to his gaining such a brilliant wife in the first place); while with Hamlet it is indecision. Seeing both sides of every argument and questioning the validity of your own motives can be a strength but Hamlet takes it too far.

1 ● Macbeth

Quote: *'Double, double, toil and trouble;*
fire burn and cauldron bubble.'

Dramatis Personae

1 MACBETH
2 BANQUO ⎫
3 MACDUFF ⎭ generals of the King's army
4 LADY MACBETH
5 THREE WITCHES
6 DUNCAN, King of Scotland
7 FLEANCE, son to Banquo

Macbeth takes ambition as its central pillar, as *King Lear* takes pride. The play recounts the rise of the Scottish nobleman Macbeth in the 11th century AD from leading chieftain in Scotland, through various bloody deeds, towards kingship. Egged on by both his wife and by mystical powers, he commits murder after murder, but is finally overcome by the forces of righteousness.

Three witches prophesy that Macbeth will be king and Banquo will be father to a line of kings. Lady Macbeth urges her husband to murder the King. Macbeth is crowned and, to stop the witches' prophecy being fulfilled, he hires murderers to kill Banquo and his son Fleance, but Fleance escapes. Macbeth sees the ghost of Banquo and he seeks out the witches who tell him to beware of Macduff, and repeat that descendants of Banquo will become kings.

Macbeth has Macduff's wife and children murdered; Macduff and his men besiege Macbeth's castle. Lady Macbeth commits suicide, Macduff kills Macbeth, and Malcolm, the eldest son of Duncan, becomes King.

2 ● Othello, the Moor of Venice

Quote: *'Oh beware, my Lord, of jealousy It is the green-eyed monster which doth mock the meat it feeds on.'*

Dramatis Personae

1 OTHELLO, a noble Moor in the service of the
   Venetian state
2 CASSIO, his lieutenant
3 IAGO, his servant
4 RODERIGO, a Venetian gentleman
5 DESDEMONA, daughter to Brabantio and wife to Othello
6 BIANCA, mistress to Cassio

Othello is considered by many to be Shakespeare's most personal play. It shows the marriage between the black Arab or Moor, Othello, and the white Italian Renaissance virgin Desdemona. Iago and Roderigo, in love with Desdemona, plot against Othello and his lieutenant, Cassio, by making Othello suspect Desdemona and Cassio of adultery. At the close, Othello kills Desdemona, but then realises he has been misled by his evil servant Iago. Filled with guilt and remorse, he kills himself.

The speed with which Othello becomes insanely jealous and the pressure and the violence of his emotions, have led many critics to believe that these were emotions that Shakespeare had personally experienced.

3 ● King Lear

Quote: *'How sharper than a serpent's tooth it is
to have a thankless child.'*

Dramatis Personae

1 LEAR, King of Britain
2 FOOL
3 GONERIL
4 REGAN ⎬ daughters to Lear
5 CORDELIA

King Lear, like *Cymbeline*, takes ancient Britain as its stage. The king, Lear, retires and divides his kingdom between two of his daughters, Regan and Goneril, who have won favour with him through flattery. As in *Timon of Athens*, the theme of ingratitude emerges, as the daughters compete for dominance, reject Lear, and cast him out.

Lear's other daughter, Cordelia, is married to the King of France without a dowry. Having refused to flatter her father, she has been cut out of Lear's division of the kingdom. Hearing of his plight, Cordelia brings an army from France to rescue him, but she is murdered. Lear, with the daughter to whom he had been unkind and who had tried to rescue him dead, and with those to whom he had given everything now rejecting him, goes mad and perishes.

4 ● Hamlet
Prince of Denmark

Quote: *'To be or not to be. That is the question.'*

Dramatis Personae

1   CLAUDIUS, King of Denmark
2   HAMLET, son to the late, and nephew to the present, King
3   POLONIUS, Lord Chamberlain
4   HORATIO, friend to Hamlet
5   LAERTES, son to Polonius
6   TWO CLOWNS, gravediggers
7   GHOST of Hamlet's father
8   GERTRUDE, Queen of Denmark, and mother to Hamlet
9   OPHELIA, daughter to Polonius
10 ROSENCRANTZ ⎱ Courtiers
11 GUILDENSTERN ⎰
12 FORTINBRAS, Prince of Norway

Hamlet is a revenge tragedy in which a wronged son seeks revenge against those who have committed crimes, in this case the murder of his father and the 'theft' of the crown of Denmark. What adds eternal lustre to this particular theme is that Hamlet is too intelligent to simply carry out the acts of revenge, and constantly questions his own motives. Ultimately he goes too far in questioning, and obscures rather than clarifies the situations he's trying to resolve.

Hamlet is told by the ghost of his father that he was murdered by his brother Claudius, now King. Hamlet feigns madness while plotting revenge. He organises a play depicting his father's death to confirm Claudius' guilt. While warning his mother, Hamlet kills Polonius, who is eavesdropping. Claudius sends Hamlet to England to be killed but he escapes and returns to Denmark.

Ophelia, Polonius' daughter, once loved by Hamlet, has drowned herself. The King proposes a duel between Hamlet and the son of Polonius, Laertes. Hamlet is wounded by a poisoned sword which he then takes to kill Laertes and the King. The Queen drinks poisoned wine prepared for Hamlet, and Hamlet dies from his own wound.

The Comedies

Shakespeare's comedies are heavily based on the standard Italian form of the *Commedia del Arte*, frequently involving twins, lookalikes, brothers and sisters, cross-dressing and mistaken identities. Naturally Shakespeare injects his own element of genius into the pre-existing plots.

1 • The Comedy of Errors

Quote: *'Am I in Earth, in Heaven or in Hell, sleeping or waking, mad or well advised?'*

Dramatis Personae

1 SOLINUS, DUKE OF EPHESUS
2 AEGEON, a merchant of Syracuse
3 ANTIPHOLUS OF EPHESUS ⎱ twin brothers, and sons
4 ANTIPHOLUS OF SYRACUSE ⎰ of Aegeon and Aemilia
5 DROMIO OF EPHESUS ⎱ twin brothers, and attendants
6 DROMIO OF SYRACUSE ⎰ on the two Antipholuses
7 AEMILIA, wife to Aegeon, an abbess at Ephesus
8 ADRIANA, wife to Antipholus of Ephesus
9 LUCIANA, her sister

The Comedy of Errors, based on Plautus's *Menaechmi*, is a delightful tale of twins, more twins, brothers and sisters, wives and lovers, all of whom become intriguingly intertwined in a series of playful misidentifications and misunderstandings.

The play primarily revolves around the two Antipholus twins, one of whom wanders away from home as a boy, and whose father consequently dies of grief.

The boy lives, grows up and marries, and the story begins with him having stolen his wife's cloak to give to his mistress. At the same time his brother arrives, looking for his lost twin.

At this point, the mistress mistakes the twin for her lover and the plot becomes wonderfully complex, with the brother having the cloak, and also meeting his brother's wife. When the original brother returns he is locked out of both his lover's and his wife's houses. However, just in time, the two brothers are seen together and the reason for the confusion is evident. They are happily reunited and go to live in Syracuse.

2 ● The Taming of the Shrew

Quote: *'For I am he am born to tame you, Kate, and bring you from a wild Kate to a Kate conformable as other household Kates.'*

Dramatis Personae

1 BAPTISTA MINOLA, a rich gentleman of Padua
2 PETRUCHIO, a gentleman of Verona, a suitor to Katharina
3 KATHARINA, the shrew ⎱ daughters to Baptista
4 BIANCA ⎰
5 LUCENTIO, son to Vincentio, in love with Bianca

A satire on relationships between men and women. Bianca is not allowed to marry until her bad-tempered elder sister, Kate, is married. Her father, Baptista, looks for tutors for Bianca and suitors for Katharina. The young Lucentio falls in love with Bianca, disguises himself as a tutor, and they secretly elope.

Kate is a frightful shrew who beats every man she meets into submission and refuses to entertain even the idea of marriage. Petruchio, a gentleman of Verona, who is prepared to marry anyone for money, gradually 'tames' Kate in a series of what might now be considered quite chauvinistic manoeuvres. At the end of the play the two achieve marital balance and harmony.

3 ● The Two Gentlemen of Verona

Quote: *'How use doth breed a habit in a man.'*

Dramatis Personae

1 DUKE OF MILAN, father to Silvia
2 VALENTINE ⎱ the two Gentlemen
3 PROTEUS   ⎰
4 ANTONIO, father to Proteus
5 JULIA, beloved of Proteus
6 SILVIA, beloved of Valentine

The Two Gentlemen of Verona is a standard romance, where love is subjected to strain from without and within. Antonio, father of Proteus, demands that his son separate from his mistress, and then Antonio falls prey to a momentary sensual attraction.

Valentine, the other 'gentleman', is banished by the duke for 'indiscreet' behaviour. The play focuses on the conflict between the men created by the demands of friendship and their various sexual attractions. After increasing difficulties, Valentine finally restores Proteus to his own favour, even offering him his own mistress.

4 ● Love's Labour's Lost

Quote: *'They have been at a great feast of languages and stolen the scraps.'*

Dramatis Personae

1 FERDINAND, KING OF NAVARRE
2 BEROWNE
3 LONGAVILLE ⎫ lords attending on the King
4 DUMAIN   ⎭
5 THE PRINCESS OF FRANCE
6 ROSALINE
7 MARIA   ⎬ ladies attending on the Princess
8 KATHARINE ⎭

Ferdinand, King of Navarre, persuades three of his courtiers, Berowne, Longaville and Dumain, to abstain from the company of women for three years. But the arrival of a French Princess and her entourage causes problems, as they each fall in love: Berowne with Rosaline; the King with the Princess; Longaville with Maria; and Dumain with Katharine.

Love poems are sent and tricks are played, but news of the French King's death necessitates the ladies' return to France. They promise that, after their period of mourning, they will return if, in between, the four men spend their time doing good deeds.

5 • A Midsummer Night's Dream

Quote: *'Methought I was enamour'd of an ass.'*

Dramatis Personae

1 THESEUS, Duke of Athens
2 LYSANDER ⎫ in love with Hermia
3 DEMETRIUS ⎭
4 BOTTOM, a weaver
5 HERMIA, daughter to Egeus, in love with Lysander
6 HELENA, in love with Demetrius
7 OBERON, King of the fairies
8 TITANIA, Queen of the fairies
9 PUCK, or Robin Goodfellow
10 HIPPOLYTA, Queen of the Amazons, betrothed to Theseus

A Midsummer Night's Dream is a witty examination of the mysterious relationships between men and women. It shows how love can be both rational and irrational at the same time.

Theseus, Duke of Athens, is to marry Hippolyta, Queen of the Amazons. Hermia refuses to give up her lover, Lysander, to marry Demetrius, and they flee to a wood, pursued by Demetrius. Demetrius, in turn, is followed by Helena, whom he has slighted in love.

In the wood, a lot of tomfoolery goes on, with Oberon casting spells on Titania and Puck playing tricks on Bottom. The play shows how romantic affections can attach themselves to the most ridiculous objects, as when Titania falls in love with an ass, who is really Bottom in disguise.

As the play ends, the magical threads are unravelled, reality returns, and all the characters go back to Athens for a triple wedding, at which the play *Pyramus and Thisbe* is enacted.

6 • Much Ado About Nothing

Quote: *'For there was never yet philosopher who could endure the toothache patiently.'*

Dramatis Personae

1 DON PEDRO, Prince of Aragon
2 DON JOHN, his bastard brother
3 BENEDICK, a young lord of Padua
4 DOGBERRY, a constable
5 LEONATO, Governor of Messina
6 BEATRICE, niece to Leonato
7 HERO, daughter to Leonato
8 CLAUDIO, a young lord of Florence

Much Ado About Nothing is a comedy of manners. Don Pedro, Prince of Aragon, and two friends, Claudio and Benedick, stay in Messina with Leonato, the Governor. Don Pedro agrees to woo Leonato's daughter, Hero, on Claudio's behalf. Meanwhile Don Pedro, Leonato and Claudio plot to bring Beatrice, Leonato's niece, and Benedick together.

Hero is alleged to be unfaithful and Claudio denounces her, but the conspirators who planned this are discovered. For distrusting Hero, Benedick and Leonato both challenge Claudio to a duel but Claudio repents. All ends well and there is a double wedding: Claudio and Hero, Beatrice and Benedick.

The play could be said to revolve around Beatrice and Benedick, who, although under the surface deeply in love, spend most of their time squabbling and using their sharp wits at each other's expense. However, when the petty squabblings and 'nothing' threaten to become a real danger to their community, they put aside their differences and are happily united.

7 ● As You Like It

Quote: *'All the world's a stage and all the men and women merely players.'*

Dramatis Personae

1 DUKE SENIOR, living in banishment
2 FREDERICK, his brother and usurper of his dominions
3 JAQUES, a banished duke
4 TOUCHSTONE, a clown
5 ROSALIND, daughter to the banished Duke
6 CELIA, daughter to Frederick

As You Like It is a charming rustic comedy in which a deposed duke, Senior, living in the forest as an outcast, hopes to reunite various lovers. In witty political and family intrigues, the lovers assume various disguises, including that of Rosalind who disguises herself as a man, causing all sorts of humorous complications. After much hilarious confusion, so typical of Shakespeare, the real relationships are all clarified, true love finds a way, and the play ends with four weddings.

8 • The Merry Wives Of Windsor

Quote: *'The world's mine oyster.'*

Dramatis Personae

1 SIR JOHN FALSTAFF
2 FENTON, a gentleman
3 FORD ⎱ two gentlemen dwelling at Windsor
4 PAGE ⎰
5 MISTRESS FORD
6 MISTRESS PAGE
7 MISTRESS QUICKLY, servant to Doctor Caius

It is said that Shakespeare wrote this play because Queen Elizabeth I was so charmed by the old rogue Falstaff in the *Henry IV* plays that she demanded a reappearance. The story is about life in the comfortable, self-assured community of Windsor where daughters Page and Ford, enterprising and independent young women, are actively involved in seeking husbands. Enter Falstaff, who arrives short of funds as usual and attempts to earn some necessary cash by means of the wives of various local citizens. Like many of Shakespeare's comedies, the play interweaves the multiple threads of relationships, involving all the representative characters of the community: two professional men, a doctor and a parson, the host of the inn and a born gossip.

The play recounts false jealousies on the part of husbands who think they are being cuckolded. Falstaff is eventually thrown into the river in a laundry basket and becomes the butt of their humour, wearing a pair of antlers (cuckold's horns) in a midnight ceremony in Windsor forest.

9 • Twelfth Night
Or, What You Will

Quote: 'Some *men are born great, some achieve greatness and some have greatness thrust upon them.'*

Dramatis Personae

1 ORSINO, DUKE OF ILLYRIA
2 OLIVIA
3 VIOLA
4 SEBASTIAN, brother to Viola
5 SIR TOBY BELCH, uncle to Olivia
6 SIR ANDREW AGUECHEEK
7 MALVOLIO, steward to Olivia
8 FESTE, A CLOWN

Like *The Two Gentlemen of Verona* and *A Midsummer Night's Dream*, *Twelfth Night* is a comedy of manners in which various lovers go through mistaken identities and multiple confusions. In the play certain types of people are held up for ridicule, such as Malvolio, the pompous servant, who takes life far too seriously and ends up being imprisoned and tormented by what he thinks are ghosts. We also see conniving servants, lords who believe themselves to be in love, and ladies who are in love with the 'wrong' person.

Twelfth Night also includes a Falstaffian character in the person of Sir Toby Belch, a hard-drinking, duelling roisterer. As with all Shakespeare's comedies, the play ends with everything happily resolved and all the characters going merrily on their way.

10 ▪ All's Well That Ends Well
Quote: *'They say miracles are past.'*

Dramatis Personae

1 KING OF FRANCE
2 BERTRAM, Count of Rousillon
3 COUNTESS OF ROUSILLON, mother to Bertram
4 HELENA, a gentlewoman protected by the Countess

This play, the last of Shakespeare's comedies, actually marks a transition between the comedy plays and the moral plays, and is often thought of as a 'dark comedy' or 'problem play'. It is full of issues that can tax and vex the mind. It is a love story, although not full of happiness. It does, however, end as well as it can. Helena is rejected by Bertram on the grounds of her inferior class, while the King speaks rationally and passionately about the value of merit over birth.

The scene begins with Helena beginning her 'cure'. This is a 'bed trick' where she must trick her husband into making love to her without him knowing it is her. This she does, but although she becomes pregnant, he loves the 'shadow' of her and there is no firm close or resolution.

The Moral Plays

Not pure comedies, not pure tragedies, but with elements of both. In these plays moral dilemmas are explored, confronting the audience with the question: 'What would I do in this situation?'

1 • Romeo and Juliet

Quote: *'Oh Romeo, Romeo, wherefore art thou Romeo?'*
'What's in a name? That which we call a rose by any other name would smell as sweet.'

Dramatis Personae

1 PARIS, a young nobleman
2 MONTAGUE ⎫ heads of two houses at
3 CAPULET ⎭ variance with each other
4 ROMEO, son to Montague
5 MERCUTIO, friend to Romeo
6 TYBALT, nephew to Lady Capulet
7 FRIAR LAURENCE, Franciscan
8 JULIET, daughter to Capulet
9 NURSE to Juliet

Two rival families, the Montagues and the Capulets, vie for pre-eminence in Renaissance Italy.

Paris, a young nobleman, has asked to marry Juliet, Capulet's 13-year-old daughter, but has been told that she is far too young.

Romeo, the son of Montague, goes to a Capulet party in disguise, and meets Juliet. They fall in love and secretly get married, but Romeo is banished after a family fight in which his friend Mercutio and the Capulet Tybalt are killed.

Amid the growing tension, Capulet changes his mind and insists that Paris and Juliet must be married within two days. Distraught but cleverly scheming, Juliet takes a potion which gives her the appearance of death. Romeo, discovering her, believes that she is dead and poisons himself. On waking, Juliet discovers the dead Romeo by her side and kills herself. The tragedy of their untimely deaths finally reconciles the families and brings peace to the town.

2 • The Merchant of Venice

Quote: *'The quality of mercy is not strained.*
It droppeth as the gentle rain from heaven.'

Dramatis Personae

1 ANTONIO, a merchant of Venice
2 SHYLOCK, a rich Jew
3 JESSICA, daughter to Shylock
4 LORENZO, in love with Jessica
5 BASSANIO, Lorenzo's friend, suitor to Portia
6 PORTIA, a rich heiress
7 NERISSA, Portia's maid

The Merchant of Venice is essentially a disquisition on the theme of mercy and compassion in human relationships.

To try to win the hand of Portia, Bassanio borrows money from his friend Antonio, who has to borrow that money from Shylock, a Jewish money-lender. Antonio agrees that, if it is not repaid within three months, Shylock can remove a pound in weight from Antonio's flesh.

Shylock's daughter, Jessica, elopes with Lorenzo, a Gentile, and Bassanio marries Portia.

Antonio's ships run aground, which means he cannot repay his loan. Shylock demands his pound of flesh. Disguised as a young lawyer and clerk, Portia and Nerissa, her maid, win Antonio's case in court. Shylock loses all and, on Antonio's insistence, becomes a Christian. Antonio's ships are happily saved.

3 ◦ Measure for Measure

Quote: *'Liberty plucks justice by the nose.'*

Dramatis Personae

1 VINCENTIO, the Duke
2 ANGELO, the Deputy
3 CLAUDIO, a young gentleman
4 ISABELLA, sister to Claudio
5 MARIANA, betrothed to Angelo

Measure for Measure is a subtle investigation into the nature of justice and whether or not justice is absolute or can be tempered with mercy. It holds up a revealing mirror to human nature.

In the play Duke Vincentio leaves his deputy, Angelo, in charge of Vienna, but disguises himself as a friar in order to keep an eye on things. Angelo starts a vindictive 'clean-up' campaign, including sentencing a young gentleman, Claudio, to the death penalty for fornication.

Isabella, Claudio's sister, who is about to enter a nunnery, pleads with Angelo to have mercy.

Angelo falls madly in love with Isabella, and offers to spare Claudio if she will give herself to him. The 'friar' has, however, been observing all these events. At his suggestion, Isabella only pretends to accept Angelo's proposal, but sends Mariana, who is already betrothed to Angelo, in her place.

Angelo, increasingly corrupted by his power, does not keep his promise and still orders Claudio's execution. The 'moral' characters arrange for a pirate to be substituted for Claudio, and the 'returned' Duke condemns Angelo to death. Finally, showing extreme mercy, the Duke pardons both Angelo and Claudio and, having fallen in love with Isabella, while disguised as the friar, asks her to marry him.

The Last Plays

Shakespeare progresses from the view expressed in his earlier masterpieces that tragic events must always have tragic outcomes. His final plays are characterised by intelligent and humane solutions to 'at first sight' disastrous situations.

1 ◦ Cymbeline
King of Britain

Quote: *'Fear no more the heat of the sun nor
the furious winter's rages.'*

Dramatis Personae

1 CYMBELINE, King of Britain
2 CLOTEN, son to the Queen by a former husband
3 POSTHUMUS LEONATUS, a gentleman, husband to Imogen
4 IMOGEN, daughter to Cymbeline by a former Queen
5 BELARIUS, a banished lord disguised under the name of Morgan
6 GUIDERIUS ⎫ sons to Cymbeline
7 ARVIRAGUS ⎭
8 QUEEN, wife to Cymbeline

This play is set during a period when Britain was essentially no longer part of the Roman Empire but was rising as a power almost equal to that of Rome. Cymbeline opposes his daughter Imogen's marriage to Posthumus; as a result, Posthumus is banished to Italy. The Queen plots to take control of the country from Cymbeline and make Cloten, her son, king, with Imogen as his bride. She successfully schemes to have the Romans declare war on Britain.

Through the Queen's conniving, Posthumus comes to believe that Imogen has been unfaithful, and orders her killed; fortunately he is unsuccessful.

The plot thickens at the arrival of Belarius, who has lived for years in a cave after kidnapping Guiderius and Arviragus, sons of Cymbeline. In the ensuing battles Guiderius kills Cloten, the Romans are defeated and peace is restored.

In the final scenes Posthumus repents and is reconciled with Imogen; the evil Queen dies; and the King is happily reunited with his sons.

2 ● The Winter's Tale
Quote: *'Exit pursued by a bear.'*

Dramatis Personae
1 LEONTES, King of Sicilia
2 AUTOLYCUS, a rogue
3 HERMIONE, Queen to Leontes
4 PERDITA, daughter to Leontes and Hermione
5 POLIXENES, King of Bohemia
6 FLORIZEL, Prince of Bohemia

The Winter's Tale has some similarities to *Othello*. Both plays involve the theme of jealousy and a powerful man who believes his wife to be unfaithful.

In this play, the King, Leontes, believes Hermione, his wife, and Polixenes, his friend and the King of Bohemia, are having an affair. As his suspicions increase, Leontes imprisons Hermione and orders their new-born daughter to be abandoned.

The daughter, Perdita (meaning 'lost'), instead of being cast adrift and killed, is found by a shepherd and eventually returns. Similarly Leontes' wife, whom he had thought dead, and had wrongly accused, comes back to life from a pillar of stone. In the play's resolution, the kings and their children are brought together again, and Perdita and Florizel are married.

3 • The Tempest

Quote: *'Our revels now are ended.'*

Dramatis Personae

1 PROSPERO, the rightful Duke of Milan
2 FERDINAND, son to the King of Naples
3 CALIBAN, a savage and deformed slave
4 TRINCULO, a jester
5 STEPHANO, a drunken butler
6 MIRANDA, daughter to Prospero
7 ARIEL, an airy spirit
8 ALONSO, King of Naples

The Tempest is normally considered to be Shakespeare's final play, and again deals with the theme of forgiveness. The play traces the banishment of Prospero, the Duke of Milan, to a distant island, peopled only by mystical fairy spirits, and hobgoblins such as Caliban.

Prospero, using magic powers, releases a spirit, Ariel, who controls a storm, during which King Alonso (the leader of the conspiracy that abandoned Prospero and his daughter Miranda at sea) and his fellow shipmates are shipwrecked.

By magic, Prospero inveigles the usurpers of his dukedom on to the island, cleverly and subtly punishing them. However, when Ferdinand, the son of Alonso, falls in love with Miranda, Alonso gives Prospero back his dukedom and begs for forgiveness. Like the other last plays, *The Tempest* ends with a bitter-sweet reconciliation. Everyone returns to Italy.

Vocabulary:
Prefixes, Suffixes and Roots

 Preview
- Prefixes
- Suffixes
- Roots

> The use and manipulation of vocabulary is the one mental skill which,
> above all others, can be most closely correlated with general personal
> success. It is therefore essential, throughout your life, to develop this
> enticing and personally releasing ability.

This may initially seem a daunting task, but happily there is an easy way to spend a little time and gain maximum rewards. In the same way as Meccano and Lego sets use a few basic pieces to create an infinity of shapes and structures, so a vast vocabulary is based upon relatively few prefixes, suffixes and roots.

On the following pages you will find, in order, the major prefixes, suffixes and roots that are liberally sprinkled through every conversation you have, and every article and book you read.

By using SEM^3 to remember these key units of vocabulary, you will enhance your memory and your ability to increase your vocabulary and therefore your 'success quotient'. You will also increase your intelligence, because memory and vocabulary skills are two of the main elements in standard intelligence (IQ) Tests.

Prefixes

(L = Latin; G = Greek; F = French; E = English. Some sources unknown.)

Prefix	Meaning	Example
a-, an- (G)	without, not	anaerobic
ab-, abs- (L)	away, from, apart	absent
ad-, ac-, af- (L)	to, towards	advent, advance
aero-	air	aeroplane, aeronaut
amb-, ambi- (G)	both, around	ambiguous
amphi- (G)	both, around	amphitheatre
ante- (L)	before	antenatal
anti- (G)	against	antidote, antitoxic
apo- (G)	away from	apostasy
arch- (G)	chief, most important	archbishop, arch-criminal
auto- (G)	self	automatic, autocrat
be-	about, make	belittle, beguile, beset
bene- (L)	well, good	benediction
bi- (G)	two	biennial, bicycle
by, bye- (G)	added to	byways, bye-laws
cata- (G)	down	catalogue, cataract
centi-, cente- (L)	hundred	centigrade, centenary
circum- (L)	around	circumference, circumambient
co-, col-, com-, cor-, con- (L)	together, with	companion, collect, co-operate
contra- (L)	against, counter	contradict, contraceptive
de- (F)	down	denude, decentralise
deca-, deci- (G)	ten	decade, decagon
demi- (L)	half	demigod
dia- (G)	through, between	diameter
dis- (L)	not, opposite to	dislike, disagree
duo- (G)	two	duologue, duplex
dys- (G)	ill, hard	dysentery
e-, ex-	out of	exhale, excavate
ec- (L)	out of	eccentric
en-, in-, em-, im- (L, G, F)	into, not	enrage, inability, embolden, emulate, impress
epi- (G)	upon, at, in addition	epidemic, epidermis
equi-	equally	equidistant
extra- (L)	outside, beyond	extramarital
for-, fore- (E)	before	foresee
hemi- (G)	half	hemisphere

Prefix	Meaning	Example
hepta- (G)	seven	heptagon
hexa- (G)	six	hexagon, hexateuch
homo- (L)	same	homonym
hyper- (G)	above, excessive	hypercritical, hypertrophy
il-	not	illegal, illogical
in-, *im-* (*un-*) (L, G, F)	not	imperfect, inaccessible
inter- (L)	among, between	interrupt, intermarriage
intra-, *intro-* (L)	inside, within	intramural, introvert
iso- (G)	equal, same	isobaric, isosceles
mal- (L)	bad, wrong	malfunction, malformed
meta- (G)	after, beyond	metabolism, metaphysical
mis-	wrongly	misfit, mislead
mono- (G)	one, single	monotonous, monocular
multi- (L)	many	multipurpose, multimillion
non-	not	nonsense, nonpareil
ob-, *oc-*, *of-*,	in the way of,	obstruct, obstacle,
op- (L)	resistance	oppose
octa-, *octo-* (G)	eight	octahedron, octave
off-	away, apart	offset
out-	beyond	outnumber, outstanding
over-	above	overhear, overcharge
para- (G)	aside, beyond	parable, paradox
penta- (G)	five	pentagon, pentateuch
per- (L)	through	perennial, peradventure
peri- (G)	around, about	perimeter, pericardium
poly- (G)	many	polygamy, polytechnic
post- (L)	after	postscript, postnatal
pre- (L)	before	prehistoric, pre-war
prime-, *primo-* (L)	first, important	primary, Prime Minister
pro- (L)	in front of, favouring	prologue, pro-British
quadri- (L)	four	quadrennial, quadrangle
re- (L)	again, back	reappear, recivilise
retro- (L)	backward	retrograde, retrospect
se-	aside	secede
self-	personalising	self-control, self-taught
semi- (G)	half	semicircle, semi-detached
sub- (L)	under	submarine, subterranean
super- (L)	above, over	superfluous, superior
syl-	with, together	syllogism
syn-, *sym-* (G)	together	sympathy, synchronise
tele- (G)	far, at or to a distance	telegram, telepathy
ter- (L)	three times	tercentenary

Prefix	Meaning	Example
tetra- (G)	four	tetrahedron, tetralogy
trans- (L)	across, through	transatlantic, translate
tri- (L, G)	three	triangle, tripartite
ultra- (L)	beyond	ultramarine, ultra-violet
un- (*im-*) (L, G, F)	not	unbroken, unbutton, unable
under-	below	underfed, underling
uni- (L)	one	unicellular, uniform
vice- (L)	in place of	viceroy, vice-president
yester- (E)	preceding time	yesterday, yesteryear

Suffixes

Suffix	Meaning	Example
-able, -ible (L)	capable of, fit for	durable, comprehensible
-acy (L, G)	state or quality of	accuracy
-age (L)	action or state of	breakage
-al, -ial (L)	relating to	abdominal
-an (-ane, -ian) (L)	the nature of	Grecian, African
-ance, -ence,	quality or action of	insurance, corpulence
-ant (L)	forming adjectives of quality, nouns signifying a personal agent or something producing an effect	defiant, servant
-arium, -orium (L)	place for	aquarium, auditorium
-ary (L)	place for, dealing with	seminary, dictionary
-atable (L)	(*see -able, -ible*)	
-ate (L)	cause to be, office of	animate, magistrate
-ation, -ition (L)	action or state of	condition, dilapidation
-cle, -icle (L)	diminutive	icicle
-dom (E)	condition or control	kingdom
-en (E)	small	mitten
-en (E)	quality	golden, broken
-er (E)	belonging to	farmer, New Yorker
-ess (E)	feminine suffix	hostess, waitress
-et, -ette (L)	small	puppet, marionette
-ferous (L)	producing	coniferous
-ful (E)	full of	colourful, beautiful
-fy, -ify (L)	make	satisfy, fortify
-hood (E)	state or condition of	boyhood, childhood
-ia (L)	names of classes, names of places	bacteria, Liberia

Suffix	Meaning	Example
-ian (L)	practitioners or inhabitants	musician, Parisian
-ible, -able, (L)	capable of, fit for	durable, comprehensible
-ic (G)	relating to	historic
-id(e) (L)	a quality	acid
-ine (G, L)	a compound	chlorine
-ion (L)	condition or action of	persuasion
-ish (E)	a similarity or relationship	childish, greenish
-ism (G)	quality or doctrine of	realism, socialism
-ist (G)	one who practises	chemist, pessimist
-itis (L)	inflammation of (medical)	bronchitis
-ity, -ety, -ty (L)	state or quality of	loyalty
-ive (L)	nature of	creative, receptive
-ize, -ise (G)	make, practise, act like	modernize, advertise
-lent (L)	fullness	violent
-less (E)	lacking	fearless, faceless
-logy (G)	indicating a branch of knowledge	biology, psychology
-ly (E)	having the quality of	softly, quickly
-ment (L)	act or condition of	resentment
-metry, -meter (G)	measurement	gasometer, geometry
-mony	resulting condition	testimony
-oid (G)	resembling	ovoid
-or (L)	a state or action, a person who, or thing which	error, governor, victor, generator
-osis	process or condition of	metamorphosis
-ous, -ose (L)	full of	murderous, anxious, officious, morose
-some	like	gladsome
-tude (L)	quality or degree of	altitude, gratitude
-ward (E)	direction	backward, outward
-y (E)	condition	difficulty

Roots

Root	Meaning	Example
aer	air	aerate, aeroplane
am (from *amare*)	love	amorous, amateur, amiable
ann (from *annus*)	year	annual, anniversary
aud (from *audire*)	hear	auditorium, audit
bio	life	biography
cap (from *capire*)	take	captive
cap (from *caput*)	head	capital, per capita, decapitate
chron	time	chronology, chronic
cor	heart	cordial
corp	body	corporation
de	god	deify, deity
dic, dict	say, speak	dictate
duc (from *ducere*)	lead	aqueduct, duke, ductile
ego	I	egotism
equi	equal	equidistant
fac, fic (from *facere*)	make, do	manufacture, efficient
frat (from *frater*)	brother	fraternity
geo	earth	geology
graph	write	calligraphy, graphology, telegraph
loc (from *locus*)	place	location, local
loqu, loc (from *loqui*)	speak	eloquence, circumlocution
luc (from *lux*)	light	elucidate
man (from *manus*)	hand	manuscript, manipulate
mit, miss (from *mittere*)	send	admit, permission
mort (from *mors*)	death	immortal
omni	all	omnipotent, omnibus
pat (from *pater*)	father	paternal
path	suffering, feeling	sympathy, pathology
ped (from *pes*)	foot	impede, millepede, pedal
phobia, phobe	fear	hydrophobe, xenophobia
photo	light	photography
pneum	air, breath, spirit	pneumonla
pos, posit	place	deposit, position
pot, poss, poten (from *ponerte*)	be able	potential, possible

Root	Meaning	Example
quaerere	question, seek	inquiry, query
rog (from *rogare*)	ask	interrogate
scrib, scrip (from *scribere*)	write	scribble, script, inscribe
sent, sens (from *sentire*)	feel	sensitive, sentient
sol	alone	soloist, isolate
soph	wise	philosopher
spect (from s*picere*)	look	introspective, inspect
spir (from *spirare*)	breathe	inspiration
ten (from *tendere*)	stretch	extend, tense
ten (from *tenere*)	hold	tenant
therm (from *thermos*)	warm	thermometer
utilis	useful	utility
ven, vent (from *venire*)	come, arrive	advent, convenient
vert, vers (from *vertere*)	turn	revert, adverse
vid, vis (from *videre*)	see	supervisor, vision, provident

Languages 14

 Preview
- Italian
- French
- German
- Spanish
- Russian
- Chinese
- Japanese

Fifty per cent of each spoken language is composed of 100 basic key words. For this reason *Master Your Memory* includes the hundred basic words from seven of the world's most common languages.

Applying SEM^3 to languages, you simply mark off one of the thousand-cross matrices, say 5000 to 5999, and apply the Memory Principles as before.

For example, let's say you were going to visit Italy, and wished to learn the first 100 words of the Italian vocabulary. If you were using the Sensation 5000 Memory Matrix, and were wanting to remember the eleventh word in the list, 'grande', which means 'big', you would take the Key Memory Image 5011, your father swimming in an Italian sea or lake. You would feel the sensations that your father feels as he swims, and envisage him with a *BIG* smile on his face because the weather is very hot, making it a *GRAND DAY* for a swim!

Memorising vocabulary in this way not only helps you memorise the words but also helps you use imagery and sensation, which are major elements in any successful language learning.

Italian

	English	Italian	Italian Pronunciation
1	A, an	Un, una	Oon, oona
2	After	Dietro	Dee-ay'troh
3	Again	Di nuovo	Dee-noo-oh'voh
4	All	Tutto	Toot'toh
5	Almost	Quasi	Kwah'zee
6	Also	Anche	Ahng'keh
7	Always	Sempre	Sem'preh
8	And	E	Ay
9	Because	Perche	Pehr'kay
10	Before	Davanti	Dah-vahn'tee
11	Big	Grande	Grahn'deh
12	But	Ma	Mah
13	Can (I can)	Io posso	Ee'oh poss-oh
14	Come (I come)	Io vengo	Ee'oh ven'go
15	Either/or	0/o	Oh/oh
16	Find (I find)	Io trovo	Ee'oh troh-voh
17	First	Primo	Pree-moh
18	For	Per	Pehr
19	Friend	Amico	Am-ee'coh
20	From	Da	Dah
21	Go (I go)	Io vado	Ee'oh vah'doh
22	Good	Buono	Boo-oh'noh
23	Goodbye	Arrivederci	Ahr-ree'veh-dehr'chee
24	Happy	Felice	Fe'lee'cheh
25	Have (I have)	Io ho	Ee'oh oh
26	He	Lui	Loo'ee
27	Hello	Ciao	Chow
28	Here	Qui	Kwee
29	How	Come	Koh'meh
30	I	Io	Ee'oh
31	I am	Sono	Soh'noh
32	If	Se	Seh
33	In	In	Een
34	Know (I know)	Io conosco	Ee'oh koh-noh-sco
35	Last	Scorso	Skorr'soh
36	Like (I like)	Mi piace	Mee pee-ah'cheh
37	Little	Poco	Poh'koh
38	Love (I love)	Io amo	Eeh'oh am'oh
39	Make (I make)	Io faccio	Ee'oh fa'choh
40	Many	Molti	Moll-tee
41	Me	Mi	Mee
42	More	Più	Pee'oo

	English	Italian	Italian Pronunciation
43	Most	Il più	Eel pee'oo
44	Much	Molto	Moll'toh
45	My	Mio	Mee'oh
46	New	Nuovo	Noo-oh'voh
47	No	No	Noh
48	Not	Non	Nonn
49	Now	Ora	Oh'rah
50	Of	Di	Dee
51	Often	Spesso	Spess'soh
52	On	Su	Soo
53	One	Uno	Oon'oh
54	Only	Solo	Soh'loh
55	Or	O	Oh
56	Other	Altro	Ahl'troh
57	Our	Il nostro	Eel noss'troh
58	Out	Fuori	Foo-oh'ree
59	Over	Attraverso	Aht'trah-vehr'soh
60	People	Gente	Jen'teh
61	Place	Luogo	Loo-oh'goh
62	Please	Per favore	Pehr fah-voh'reh
63	Same	Medesimo	Meh-day'zeemoh
64	See (I see)	Io vedo	Eeh'oh vay-doh
65	She	Lei	Lay'ee
66	So	Così	Koh'zee
67	Some	Qualche	Kwahl'keh
68	Sometimes	Talvolta	Tahl-voll'tah
69	Still	Ancora	Ahng'koh-rah
70	Such	Tale	Tah'lay
71	Tell (I tell)	Io racconto	Ee'oh rak-kon'toh
72	Thank you	Grazie	Grah'tsee-eh
73	That	Quello	Kwell'loh
74	The	Il, la	Eel, lah
75	Their	Il loro, la loro	Eel loh'roh, lah loh'roh
76	Them	Li, le, loro	Lee, lay, loh'roh
77	Then	Allora	Ahl-loh'rah
78	There is, there are	C'e, ci sono	Cheh, chee soh-noh
79	They	Loro	Loh'roh
80	Thing	Cosa	Koh'sah
81	Think (I think)	Io penso	Eeh'oh pen-soh
82	This	Questo	Kwess'toh
83	Time	Ora	Oh'rah
84	To	Per	Pehr
85	Under	Più basso	Pee-oo bahs'soh
86	Up	Su per	Soo pehr

	English	Italian	Italian Pronunciation
87	Us	Noi	Noh'ee
88	Use (I use)	Io uso	Eeh'oh oo-zoh
89	Very	Molto	Moll'toh
90	We	Noi	Noy
91	What	Come	Koh'may
92	When	Quando	Kwahn'doh
93	Where	Dove	Doh'veh
94	Which	Quale	Kwah'leh
95	Who	Chi	Kee
96	Why	Perché	Pehr-keh
97	With	Con	Kon
98	Yes	Si	See
99	You	Tu	Too
100	Your	Il suo, la sua	Eel soo'oh, lah soo'ah

French

* 'Je' is pronounced like the 'zh' sound in 'pleasure' or 'beige'. Where (n) is in brackets, it is pronounced nasally.

	English	French	French Pronunciation
1	A, an	Un, une	Er(n), oon
2	After	Après	A'pray
3	Again	Encore	O(n)'kor
4	All	Tout, toute	Too, toot
5	Almost	Presque	Press'ke
6	Also	Aussi	Oh'see
7	Always	Toujours	Too'zhure
8	And	Et	Ay
9	Because	Parce que	Pah'ske
10	Before	Avant	A'vo(n)
11	Big	Grand, Grande	Gro(n), Gro(n)d
12	But	Mais	May
13	Can (I can)	Je peux	*Je pe
14	Come (I come)	Je viens	*Je vee'a(n)
15	Either/or	Ou/ou	Ooh/ooh
16	Find (I find)	Je trouve	*Je troov
17	First	Premier	Preh'mee'ay
18	For	Pour	Poor
19	Friend	Ami, Amie	Am'ee, Am'ee
20	From	De	De
21	Go (I go)	Je vais	*Je vay
22	Good	Bien	Bee'a(n)
23	Goodbye	Au revoir	O-re'vwa

	English	French	French Pronunciation
24	Happy	Content, Contente	Ko(n)'to(n), Ko(n)'tont
25	Have (I have)	J'ai	*Jay
26	He	Il	Eel
27	Hello	Bonjour	Bo(n)'zhure
28	Here	Ici	Ee'see
29	How	Comment	Kom'o(n)
30	I	Je	*Je
31	I am	Je suis	*Je swee
32	If	Si	See
33	In	Dans	Do(n)
34	Know (I know)	Je sais	*Je say
35	Last	Dernier	Dair'nee'ay
36	Like (I like)	J'aime	*Jem
37	Little	Petit, Petite	Pe'tee, Pe'teet
38	Love (I love)	J'aime	*Jem
39	Make (I make)	Je fais	*Je fay
40	Many	Beaucoup	Bo'ku
41	Me	Moi	Mwa
42	More	Plus	Ploo
43	Most	La plupart	La ploo'par
44	Much	Beaucoup	Bo'ku
45	My	Mon, Ma	Mo(n), Ma
46	New	Nouveau, nouvelle	Nu'vo, nu'vel
47	No	Non	No(n)
48	Not	Ne pas	Ne pah
49	Now	Maintenant	Ma(n)'te'no(n)
50	Of	De	De
51	Often	Souvent	Soo'von(n)
52	On	Sur	S'ure
53	One	Un, Une	Er(n), Oon
54	Only	Seulement	Serl'e'mo(n)
55	Or	Ou	Ooh
56	Other	Autre	Oh'tr
57	Our	Notre	No'tr
58	Out	Dehors	De'or
59	Over	Pardessus	Par'de'soo
60	People	Les gens	Lay *jo(n)
61	Place	Place	Plas
62	Please	S'il vous plaît	Seel voo play
63	Same	Même	Memm
64	See (I see)	Je vois	*Je vwa
65	She	Elle	El
66	So	Donc	Do(n)k

	English	French	French Pronunciation
67	Some	Quelque	Kel'ke
68	Sometimes	Quelquefois	Kel'ke fwa
69	Still	Encore	O(n)'kor
70	Such	Tel	Tell
71	Tell (I tell)	Je dis	*Je dee
72	Thank you	Merci	Mair'see
73	That	Que	Ke
74	The	Le, la	Le, lah
75	Their	Leur	Ler
76	Them	Les	Lay
77	Then	Alors	Ah-loh're
78	There is, there are	Il y a	Eel ee ar
79	They	Ils, elles	Eel, ell
80	Thing	Chose	Sh'ohs
81	Think (I think)	Je pense	*Je po(n)se
82	This	Ce, cette	Se, set
83	Time	Temps	To(n)
84	To	A	Ah
85	Under	Sous	Soo
86	Up	En haut	On'oh
87	Us	Nous	Noo
88	Use (I use)	J'utilise	*Joo'tee'lees
89	Very	Très	Tray
90	We	Nous	Noo
91	What	Que	Ke
92	When	Quand	Ko(n)
93	Where	Où	Ooh
94	Which	Quel, quelle	Kel, kel
95	Who	Qui	Kee
96	Why	Pourquoi	Poor kwah
97	With	Avec	A'vek
98	Yes	Oui	Wee
99	You	Tu, vous	Too, voo
100	Your	Ton, tes, votre, vos	To(n), tay, vot're, voh

German

Pronunciation: 'w' is pronounced as 'v', and v' is pronounced as 'f', 'g' as in 'goat', 'k' as in 'loch', 'ü' as in 'soon' and 'u' as in 'foot'.

	English	German	German Pronunciation
1	A, an	Ein, eine	Ine, i-ne
2	After	Nach	Nahk
3	Again	Wieder	Vee-dair

	English	German	German Pronunciation
4	All	Alle	Ul-le
5	Almost	Beinahe	By-nah
6	Also	Auch	Owk
7	Always	Immer	Im'me
8	And	Und	Oont
9	Because	Weil	Vile
10	Before	Vorne	Fawrne
11	Big	Gross	Grohs
12	But	Aber	Ar'be
13	Can (I can)	Ich kann	Ik kan
14	Come (I come)	Ich komme	Ik komm'e
15	Either/or	Entweder/oder	Ent'vay'der/oh'der
16	Find (I find)	Ich finde	Ik fin'de
17	First	Erst	Air'st
18	For	Für	Fewr
19	Friend	Freund	Froynt
20	From	Von	Fon
21	Go (I go)	Ich gehe	Ik gay'e
22	Good	Gut	Goot
23	Goodbye	Auf wiedersehen	Owf' vee'dair-zay-en
24	Happy	Glücklich	Glewk'lik
25	Have (I have)	Ich habe	Ik hah'be
26	He	Er	Air
27	Hello	Guten tag	Goot'en tahg
28	Here	Hier	Heer
29	How	Wie	Vee
30	I	Ich	Ik
31	I am	Ich bin	Ik bin
32	If	Wenn	Ven
33	In	In	In
34	Know (I know)	Ich weiss	Ik vice
35	Last	Letzt	Let's't
36	Like (I like)	Ich mag	Ik mahg
37	Little	Klein	Kline
38	Love (I love)	Ich liebe	Ik lee'be
39	Make (I make)	Ich mache	Ik mu'ke
40	Many	Viel	Feel
41	Me	Mich	Mik
42	More	Mehr	M'air
43	Most	Die meisten	Dee my'sten
44	Much	Viel	Feel
45	My	Mein	Mine
46	New	Neu	Noy
47	No	Nein	Nine

	English	German	German Pronunciation
48	Not	Nicht	Nikt
49	Now	Jetzt	Yet's't
50	Of	Von	Fon
51	Often	Oft	Off't
52	On	Auf	Owf
53	One	Ein	Ine
54	Only	Nur	Newr
55	Or	Oder	O'de
56	Other	Andere	Un'de're
57	Our	Unser	Oon'sair
58	Out	Aus	Ows
59	Over	Über	Oo'bair
60	People	Leute	Loy'te
61	Place	Platz	Plahts
62	Please	Bitte	Bitter
63	Same	Derselbe, dieselbe, dasselbe	Dair'sel'be dee'sel'be duss'sel'be
64	See (I see)	Ich sehe	Ik say'e
65	She	Sie	Zee
66	So	So	Zoh
67	Some	Etwas	Et'vahss
68	Sometimes	Manchmal	Monk'mahl
69	Still	Noch	Nok
70	Such	Solch	Solk
71	Tell (I tell)	Ich erzähle	Ik air'zay'le
72	Thank you	Danke	Dahnn'ke
73	That	Das, dass	Duss
74	The	Der, die, das	Dair, dee, duss
75	Their	Ihr	Eer
76	Them	Sie	Zee
77	Then	Dann	Dahnn
78	There is, There are	Es gibt	Ess gib't
79	They	Sie	Zee
80	Thing	Die Sache	Dee sah'ke
81	Think (I think)	Ich denke	Ik den'ke
82	This	Diese	Dee'ze
83	Time	Zeit	Tsite
84	To	Nach	Nahk
85	Under	Unter	Oon'te
86	Up	Auf	Ow'f
87	Us	Uns	Oon's
88	Use (I use)	Ich gebrauche	Ik gay'brow'ke
89	Very	Sehr	Zare
90	We	Wir	Veer

91	What	Was	Vahss
92	When	Wann	Vun
93	Where	Wo	Voh
94	Which	Welche	Vel'ke
95	Who	Wer	Vair
96	Why	Warum	Var'oom
97	With	Mit	Mitt
98	Yes	Ja	Yah
99	You	Du, sie	Doo, zee
100	Your	Ihr, eure	Ear, oy'er

Spanish

	English	Spanish	Spanish Pronunciation
1	A, an	Un, uno, una	Oon, oo'no, oo'na
2	After	Después	Days-pues
3	Again	De nuevo	Day nway'vo
4	All	Todo	To'do
5	Almost	Casi	Ka'see
6	Also	También	Tam-byayn
7	Always	Siempre	Syem'pray
8	And	Y	Ee
9	Because	Porque	Por'kay
10	Before	Ante	An'tay
11	Big	Grande	Gran'day
12	But	Pero	Pay'ro
13	Can (I can)	Puedo	Pway'do
14	Come (I come)	Vengo	Ven'go
15	Either/or	O/o	Oh/oh
16	Find (I find)	Encuentro	En-kwen'tro
17	First	Primero	Pree-may'ro
18	For	Por	Por
19	Friend	Amigo	Ah'mee'go
20	From	De	Day
21	Go (I go)	Voy	Voy
22	Good	Bueno	Bway'no
23	Goodbye	Adiós	Ah'dyos
24	Happy	Contento	Con'ten'to
25	Have (I have)	Tengo	Tayn-go
26	He	El	Ell
27	Hello	Buenas días	Bway'nas dee'as
28	Here	Aquí	Ah-kee
29	How	Cómo	Ko'mo
30	I	Yo	Yo
31	I am	Soy	Soy
32	If	Si	See

	English	Spanish	Spanish Pronunciation
33	In	En	En
34	Know (I know)	Sabo	Sa-bo
35	Last	Último	Ool'tee-mo
36	Like (I like)	Gusto	Goos-to
37	Little	Poco	Po'ko
38	Love (I love)	Amo	Ah'mo
39	Make (I make)	Hago	Ar'go
40	Many	Muchos	Moo'chos
41	Me	Me	May
42	More	Más	MaHs
43	Most	Lo más	Lo maHs
44	Much	Mucho	Moo'cho
45	My	Mi	Mee
46	New	Nuevo	Nway'vo
47	No	No	No
48	Not	No	No
49	Now	Ahora	A-o'ra
50	Of	De	Day
51	Often	Frecuentemente	Fray-kwen'tay' men'tay
52	On	Sobre	So'bray
53	One	Uno	Oo'no
54	Only	Solo	So'lo
55	Or	O	O
56	Other	Otro	O'tro
57	Our	Nuestro	Nway'stro
58	Out	Fuera	Fway'ra
59	Over	Sobre	So'bray
60	People	Gente	Hen'tay
61	Place	Lugar	Loo-gar
62	Please	Por favor	Por fa'vor
63	Same	Mismo	Mees'mo
64	See (I see)	Veo	Vay'o
65	She	Ella	El'lya
66	So	Así	Ah-see
67	Some	Algun	Al-goon
68	Sometimes	Algunas veces	Al-goo'nas vaythes
69	Still	Siempre	Syem'pray
70	Such	Tal	Tal
71	Tell (I tell)	Digo	Dee'go
72	Thank you	Gracias	Gra'thyas
73	That	Ese	Ay'say
74	The	El, la, lo	El, lah, loh
75	Their	Su, sus	Soo, soos
76	Them	Los, las, les	Los, lahss, lays

	English	Spanish	Spanish Pronunciation
77	Then	Luego	Lway'go
78	There is, there are	Hay	Aye
79	They	Ellos, ellas	Ay'lyos, Ay'lyahss
80	Thing	Cosa	Ko'sa
81	Think (I think)	Pienso	Pyayn-so
82	This	Este, esta	Ays'tay, ays'tah
83	Time	Tiempo	Tyem'po
84	To	A	Ah
85	Under	Debajo	Day-ba'ho
86	Up	Arriba	Ah-ree'ba
87	Us	Nos	Nohs
88	Use (I use)	Uso	00'so
89	Very	Muy	Mwee
90	We	Nosotros	Nohs'ot'rohs
91	What	Lo que	Lo kay
92	When	Cuando	Kwan'do
93	Where	Dónde	Kwan'do
94	Which	Que	Kay
95	Who	Quién	Kee'en
96	Why	Porque	Por'kay
97	With	Con	Kon
98	Yes	Sí	See
99	You	Tu	Too
100	Your	Suyo	Soo'yo

Russian

Pronunciation at the end of the stressed syllable:

kh	as in loch	eh as in hair	
zh	as in pleasure	o as in dock	
a	as in car	oh as in order	
e	as in bet	uh as in duck	
ooi	a single sound with the emphasis on the 'i'		

	English	Russian	Russian Pronunciation
1	A, an	–	–
2	After	Posle	Poh'slye
3	Again	Eshche	Yesh-cho'
4	All	Vse	Fsye
5	Almost	Pochti	Puhch-tee'
6	Also	Tozhe	Toh'zhe
7	Always	Vsegda	Fsyeg-da'
8	And	I	Ee
9	Because	Potomu chto	Puh-tuh-moo'shto
10	Before	Do	Doh

	English	Russian	Russian Pronunciation
11	Big	Bolshoi	Buhl-shoi
12	But	No	No
13	Can (I can)	Ya mogu	Ya muh-goo
14	Come (I come)	Ya pridu	Yah pree-doo
15	Either/or	lli/ili	Ee'li/ee'li
16	Find (I find)	Ya naidu	Ya nuhee-doo
17	First	Pervyi	Pyehr'vooi
18	For	Dlya	Dlyah
19	Friend	Dryg	Droog
20	From	Ot	Ot
21	Go (I go)	Ya idu	Ya ee-doo'
22	Good	Khorosho	Khu-ruh-shoh'
23	Goodbye	Do svidaniya	Duh-svi-dan'yuh
24	Happy	Schastlivyi	Schuhst-lee'vooi
25	Have (I have)	Ya imeyu	Ya eem-yay'yoo
26	He	On	Ohn
27	Hello	Sdravstvuite	Zdrafst'vooi-tye
28	Here	Zdes	Zdyays
29	How	Kak	Kak
30	I	Ya	Yah
31	I am	Ya	Yah
32	If	Esli	Yasy'lee
33	In	V	V
34	Know (I know)	Ya znayu	Yah znaee'yoo
35	Last	Poslednii	Puh'slyay'dnee
36	Like (I like)	Mne nravitsya	Mnye nra'vi-tsyuh
37	Little	Malenkii	Ma'lyen-kee
38	Love (I love)	Ya lyublyu	Ya lyoob-lyoo'
39	Make (I make)	Ya delayu	Ya dyehl'yoo
40	Many	Mnogo	Mnoh'goh
41	Me	Menya	Men-yah
42	More	Bolshe	Bol'she
43	Most	Nai-bolshii	Nai-bol'shee
44	Much	Mnogo	Mnoh'goh
45	My	Moi	Mo'ee
46	New	Novyi	Noh'vooee
47	No	Net	Nyet
48	Not	Ne	Nye
49	Now	Teper	Tye-pyehr'
50	Of	Iz	Is
51	Often	Chasto	Chuh'stoh
52	On	Na	Nah
53	One	Odin	Uh-deen
54	Only	Tolko	Tohl'koh
55	Or	Ili	Ee'li

	English	Russian	Russian Pronunciation
56	Other	Drugoi	Droo-goy
57	Our	Nash	Nahsh
58	Out	Iz	Is
59	Over	Nad	Nahd
60	People	Lyudi	Lyoo'dee
61	Place	Mesto	Myes'tuh
62	Please	Pozhaluista	Puh-zhahl'stah
63	Same	Samyi	Sahm'ooee
64	See (I see)	Ya vizhu	Yah vee'zhoo
65	She	Ona	Uh-nah
66	So	Tak	Tuhk
67	Some	Nekotoryi	Nye'kuh-to-rooi
68	Sometimes	Inogda	Ee-nuhg-dah
69	Still	Eschcho	Yesh-choh'
70	Such	Takoi	Tuh-koy
71	Tell (I tell)	Ya skazhu	Yaskuh-zhoo'
72	Thank you	Spasibo	Spuh-see'buh
73	That	Etot	Eh'tuht
74	The	–	–
75	Their	Ikh	Eekh
76	Them	Ikh	Eekh
77	Then	Togda	Tuhg-dah
78	There is, There are	Est	Yest
79	They	Oni	Uh-nee
80	Thing	Predmet	Pryed-myet'
81	Think (I think)	Ya dumayu	Yah doo'mah-yoo
82	This	Etot	Eh'tuht
83	Time	Vremya	Vry-ay'myuh
84	To	Na	Nah
85	Under	Pod	Pod
86	Up	Naverkh	Nah-vehrkh
87	Us	Nas	Nahs
88	Use (I use)	Ya ispolzuyu	Ya is-pol'zoo-yoo
89	Very	Ochen	Oh'chen
90	We	Myi	Mooee
91	What	Chto	Shtoh
92	When	Kogda	Kuhg-dah
93	Where	Gde	Gdye
94	Which	Kakoi	Kuh-koi'
95	Who	Kto	Ktoh
96	Why	Pochemu	Puh-che-moo'
97	With	S	S
98	Yes	Da	Dah
99	You	Vyi	Vooee
100	Your	Vash	Vahsh

Chinese

Pronunciation:

ow	as in cow	er	as in her
ih	as in high	ir	as in sir
g	as an initial is hard		

	English	Chinese	Chinese (Pin Yin) Pronunciation
1	A, an	Yi, ge	Ee, ger
2	After	Guo le	Gwo ler
3	Again	You	Yoh
4	All	Dou	Doh
5	Almost	Cha bu duo	Chah boo dwoh
6	Also	Hai	High
7	Always	Yong yuan	Yung yooen
8	And	He	Her
9	Because	Yin wei	Yin way
10	Before	Yi gian	Ee chyen
11	Big	Da	Dah
12	But	Ke shi	Ker shir
13	Can (I can)	Ke yi	Ke ee
14	Come (I come)	Wo lai	Woh lih
15	Either/or	Huo zhe	Hwoh je
16	Find (I find)	Wo zhao dao	Woh jow dao
17	First	Di yi	Dee ee
18	For	Wei	Way
19	Friend	Peng you	Pung yo
20	From	Cong	Tsong
21	Go (I go)	Wo qu	Woh chew
22	Good	Hao	How
23	Goodbye	Zai jian	Dzih jyen
24	Happy	Gao xing	Gow sing
25	Have (I have)	Wo you	Woh yo
26	He	Ta	Tah
27	Hello	Ni hao	Nee ow
28	Here	Zhe li	Jer lee
29	How	Zen me	Dzen mer
30	I	Wo	Woh
31	I am	Wo shi	Woh she
32	If	Ru guo	Rroo gwoh
33	In	Li	Lee
34	Know (I know)	Wo zhi dao	Woh jir dow
35	Last	Zui hou	Dzway hoh
36	Like (I like)	Wo xi huan	Woh see hwan
37	Little	Xiao	Seeow
38	Love (I love)	Wo ai	Woh ih

	English	Chinese	Chinese (Pin Yin) Pronunciation
39	Make (I make)	Wo zhi zao	Wo jir dzow
40	Many	Duo	Dwoh
41	Me	Wo	Woh
42	More	Geng duo de	Geung dwor der
43	Most	Zui duo	Dzway dwoh
44	Much	Duo	Dwoh
45	My	Wo de	Woh de
46	New	Xin	Sin
47	No	Bu	Boo
48	Not	Bu shi	Boo shir
49	Now	Xian zai	See'en tsih
50	Of	De	De
51	Often	Jing chang	Jing chung
52	On	Shang	Shung
53	One	Yi	Ee
54	Only	Zhi	Je
55	Or	Huo zhe	Hwor jer
56	Other	Bie de	Beeye de
57	Our	Wo men de	Woh men de
58	Out	Wai	Wih
59	Over	Shang	Shung
60	People	Ren min	Ren min
61	Place	Di fang	Dee fang
62	Please	Qing	Ching
63	Same	Tong	Tung
64	See (I see)	Wo kan jian	Woh kan jyen
65	She	Ta	Tah
66	So	Suo yi	Soowoh ee
67	Some	Yi xie	Ee sye
68	Sometimes	You shi huo	Yoh she hwoh
69	Still	Hai	Hih
70	Such	Na me	Nah me
71	Tell (I tell)	Wo gao su	Woh gow soo
72	Thank you	Xie xie	Sye sye
73	That	Na ge	Nah ge
74	The	–	–
75	Their	Ta men de	Tah men de
76	Them	Ta men	Tah men
77	Then	Ran Hou	Rran hoh
78	There is, There are	You	Yoh
79	They	Ta men	Tah men
80	Thing	Dong Xi	Dung see
81	Think (I think)	Xiang	Seeyang
82	This	Zhei ge	Jay ge
83	Time	Shi jian	She jen

	English	Chinese	Chinese (Pin Yin) Pronunciation
84	To	Dao	Dow
85	Under	Xia	Seeah
86	Up	Shang	Shung
87	Us	Wo men	Woh men
88	Use (I use)	Wo yong	Woh yoong
89	Very	Hen	Hen
90	We	Wo men	Woh men
91	What	Shen me	Shen mer
92	When	Shen me shi hou	Shen mer shir ho
93	Where	Zai nar	Tsih nar
94	Which	Nei ge	Nay ger
95	Who	Shei	Shay
96	Why	Wei shi me	Way shir mer
97	With	Tong	Tung
98	Yes	Shi	She
99	You	Ni	Nee
100	Your	Ni de	Nee de

Japanese

	English	Japanese	Japanese Pronunciation
1	A, an	Hitotsu no	Hee-toh-tsoo noh
2	After	Atode	Ah-toh-deh
3	Again	Mata	Mah-tah
4	All	Minna	Meen-nah
5	Almost	Hotondo	Hoh-tohn-doh
6	Also	Mata	Mah-tah
7	Always	Itsumo	Ee-tsoo-moh
8	And	Soshite	Soh-shee-teh
9	Because	Node	Noh-deh
10	Before	Mae ni	Mah-eh nee
11	Big	Okii	Oh-kee
12	But	Keredomo	Keh-reh-doh-moh
13	Can (I can)	Dekiru	Deh-kee-doo
14	Come (I come)	Kuru	Koo-doo
15	Either/or	Ka	Kah
16	Find (I find)	Mitsukeru	Mee-tsoo-keh-doo
17	First	Hajime	Hah-jee-meh
18	For	Tamini	Tah-mee-nee
19	Friend	Tomodachi	Tomo-dar'chee
20	From	Kara	Kah-rah
21	Go (I go)	Ikimasu	Ikki'muss
22	Good	Ii	Ee
23	Goodbye	Sayonara	Sah-yoh-nah-rah

	English	Japanese	Japanese Pronunciation
24	Happy	Shiawase	Shee'a-wah'say
25	Have (I have)	Motte imasu	Moht-teh ee-mahss
26	He	Kare	Kah-deh
27	Hello	Konnichi wa	Kohn-nee-chee wah
28	Here	Koko	Koh-koh
29	How	Doshite	Doh'shtey
30	I	Watashi	Wah-tah-shee
31	I am	Watashi wa	Wah-tah-shee wah
32	If	Moshi	Moh-shee
33	In	Ni	Nee
34	Know (I know)	Shitte imasu	Sheet-teh ee-mahss
35	Last	Owari	Oh-wah-dee
36	Like (I like)	Suki	Soo-kee
37	Little	Chiisai	Chee-sah-ee
38	Love (I love)	Sukidesu	Soo'kee-dess'oo
39	Make (I make)	Shitemasu	Shih'ti-muss'oo
40	Many	Takusan	Tah-koo-sahn
41	Me	Watashi ni	Wah-tah-shee nee
42	More	Motto	Moht-toh
43	Most	Ichidan	Ee-chee-dahn
44	Much	Takusan	Tah-koo-sahn
45	My	Watashi no	Wah-tah-she noh
46	New	Atarashii	Ah-tah-dah-shee
47	No	Iie	Ee-eh
48	Not	Shinai	Shee-nah-ee
49	Now	Ima	Ee-mah
50	Of	No	Noh
51	Often	Tabitabi	Tah-bee-tah-bee
52	On	Ue	Oo-eh
53	One	Ichi	Ee-chee
54	Only	Tatta	Taht-tah
55	Or	Ka	Kah
56	Other	Hoka	Hoh-kah
57	Our	Watatshitachi no	Wah-tah-shee-tah-chee noh
58	Out	Soto	Soh-toh
59	Over	Ue	Oo-eh
60	People	Hitobito	Hee-toh-bee-toh
61	Place	Tokoro	Toh-koh-doh
62	Please	Kudasai	Koo-dah-sah-ee
63	Same	Onaji	Oh-noh-jee
64	See (I see)	Mimasu	Mee-mahss
65	She	Kanojo	Kah-noh-joh
66	So	So	Soh

	English	Japanese	Japanese Pronunciation
67	Some	Ikuraka	Ee-koo-dah-kah
68	Sometimes	Tokidoki	Toh-kee-doh-kee
69	Still	Mada	Mah-dah
70	Such	Sonna	Sohn-nah
71	Tell (I tell)	Iiamasu	Ee'muss
72	Thank you	Arigato	Ah-ree-gah-toh
73	That	Sono	Soh-noh
74	The	Sono	Soh-noh
75	Their	Karera no	Kah-deh-dah noh
76	Them	Karera no	Kah-deh-dah noh
77	Then	Dewa	Deh-wah
78	There is, there are	Soko desu	Soh-koh dess
79	They	Karera	Kah-deh-dah
80	Thing	Mono	Moh-noh
81	Think (I think)	Omou	Oh-moh-oo
82	This	Kono	Koh-noh
83	Time	Jikan	Jee-kahn
84	To	Ni	Nee
85	Under	Shita	Shee-tah
86	Up	Ue	Oo-eh
87	Us	Wareware ni	Wah-deh-wah-deh nee
88	Use (I use)	Tsukau	Tsoo-kah-oo
89	Very	Taihen	Tie-hehn
90	We	Watashitachi	Wah-tah-shee-tah-chee
91	What	Nani	Nah-nee
92	When	Itsu	Ee-tsoo
93	Where	Doko	Doh-koh
94	Which	Dore	Do're
95	Who	Donata	Do'nah'ta
96	Why	Naze	Nah'ze
97	With	De	Den
98	Yes	Hai	Hie
99	You	Anata	Ah-nah-tah
100	Your	Anata no	Ah-nah-tah noh

Countries/ Capitals 15

In a period of less than a year you will have a knowledge of the location

of the countries and capitals of the world, and of the current events

that relate to them, that will rank you, literally and mathematically,

as one in a million!

If you regularly watch or listen to the news, or subscribe to a daily newspaper, then you will be 'confronted' with the countries and capitals of the world on an almost daily basis. Despite this regular 'familiarity' with the information, most people can name no more than ten countries with their appropriate capital, and have very little idea of where each country is.

The reason for this is once again the negative spiral, in which the more you know you don't know, the more rapidly your mind becomes confused with the bombardment of new information, the less is learnt, and the more even what you *do* know eventually becomes confused.

By memorising each country and its capital, and by mentally imagining the country's location with the aid of the maps on pages 159 and 160, you will find that the more you see, hear and read about the countries and the capitals, the more you will know and remember.

	Country	Capital
1	Afghanistan	Kabul
2	Albania	Tiranë
3	Algeria	Algiers
4	Andorra	Andorra la Vella
5	Angola	Luanda
6	Antigua & Barbuda	St John's
7	Argentina	Buenos Aires
8	Armenia	Yerevan
9	Australia	Canberra
10	Austria	Vienna
11	Azerbaijan	Baku
12	Bahamas	Nassau
13	Bahrain	Manama
14	Bangladesh	Dhaka
15	Barbados	Bridgetown
16	Belarus	Minsk
17	Belgium	Brussels
18	Belize	Belmopan
19	Benin	Porto Novo
20	Bhutan	Thimphu
21	Bolivia	La Paz
22	Bosnia & Herzegovina	Sarajevo
23	Botswana	Gaborone
24	Brazil	Brasilia
25	Brunei	Bandar Seri Begawan
26	Bulgaria	Sofia
27	Burkina Faso	Ouagadougou
28	Burma	Rangoon
29	Burundi	Bujumbura
30	Cambodia	Phnom Penh
31	Cameroon	Yaoundé
32	Canada	Ottawa
33	Cape Verde	Praia
34	Central African Republic	Bangui
35	Chad	N'Djamena
36	Chile	Santiago
37	China	Beijing
38	Colombia	Bogotá
39	Comoros	Moroni
40	Congo, Republic of	Brazzaville
41	Congo, Dem. Republic of	Kinshasa
42	Costa Rica	San José
43	Côte d'Ivoire	Yamoussoukro
44	Croatia	Zagreb
45	Cuba	Havana
46	Cyprus	Nicosia
47	Czech Republic	Prague
48	Denmark	Copenhagen
49	Djibouti	Djibouti

	Country	Capital
50	Dominica	Roseau
51	Dominican Republic	Santo Domingo
52	Ecuador	Quito
53	Egypt	Cairo
54	El Salvador	San Salvador
55	Equatorial Guinea	Malabo
56	Eritrea	Asmara
57	Estonia	Tallinn
58	Ethiopia	Addis Ababa
59	Falkland Islands	Stanley
60	Fiji	Suva
61	Finland	Helsinki
62	France	Paris
63	French Guiana	Cayenne
64	Gabon	Libreville
65	Gambia	Banjul
66	Georgia	Tbilisi
67	Germany	Berlin
68	Ghana	Accra
69	Greece	Athens
70	Grenada	St George's
71	Guatemala	Guatemala City
72	Guinea	Conakry
73	Guinea-Bissau	Bissau
74	Guyana	Georgetown
75	Haiti	Port-au-Prince
76	Holy See	Vatican City
77	Honduras	Tegucigalpa
78	Hungary	Budapest
79	Iceland	Reykjavik
80	India	New Delhi
81	Indonesia	Jakarta
82	Iran	Tehran
83	Iraq	Baghdad
84	Ireland	Dublin
85	Israel	Jerusalem
86	Italy	Rome
87	Jamaica	Kingston
88	Japan	Tokyo
89	Jordan	Amman
90	Kazakhstan	Astana
91	Kenya	Nairobi
92	Kiribati	Tarawa
93	Kuwait	Kuwait
94	Kyrgyzstan	Bishkek
95	Laos	Vientiane
96	Latvia	Riga
97	Lebanon	Beirut

	Country	Capital
98	Lesotho	Maseru
99	Liberia	Monrovia
100	Libya	Tripoli
101	Liechtenstein	Vaduz
102	Lithuania	Vilnius
103	Luxembourg	Luxembourg
104	Macedonia, F.Y.R. of	Skopje
105	Madagascar	Antananarivo
106	Malawi	Lilongwe
107	Malaysia	Kuala Lumpur
108	Maldives	Malé
109	Mali	Bamako
110	Malta	Valletta
111	Marshall Islands	Majuro
112	Mauritania	Nouakchott
113	Mauritius	Port Louis
114	Mexico	Mexico City
115	Moldova	Chisinau
116	Monaco	Monaco-Ville
117	Mongolia	Ulaanbaatar
118	Morocco	Rabat
119	Mozambique	Maputo
120	Namibia	Windhoek
121	Nepal	Kathmandu
122	Netherlands	Amsterdam
123	New Zealand	Wellington
124	Nicaragua	Managua
125	Niger	Niamey
126	Nigeria	Abuja
127	North Korea	Pyongyang
128	Norway	Oslo
129	Oman	Muscat
130	Pakistan	Islamabad
131	Palau	Koror
132	Panama	Panama City
133	Papua New Guinea	Port Moresby
134	Paraguay	Asunción
135	Peru	Lima
136	Philippines	Manila
137	Poland	Warsaw
138	Portugal	Lisbon
139	Puerto Rico	San Juan
140	Qatar	Doha
141	Romania	Bucharest
142	Russia	Moscow
143	Rwanda	Kigali
144	St Kitts & Nevis	Basseterre
145	St Lucia	Castries

	Country	Capital
146	St Vincent	Kingstown
147	Samoa	Apia
148	São Tomé & Príncipe	São Tomé
149	Saudi Arabia	Riyadh
150	Senegal	Dakar
151	Serbia & Montenegro	Belgrade & Podgorica
152	Seychelles	Victoria
153	Sierra Leone	Freetown
154	Singapore	Singapore
155	Slovakia	Bratislava
156	Slovenia	Ljubljana
157	Solomon Islands	Honiara
158	Somalia	Mogadishu
159	South Africa	Pretoria
160	South Korea	Seoul
161	Spain	Madrid
162	Sri Lanka	Colombo
163	Sudan	Khartoum
164	Suriname	Paramaribo
165	Swaziland	Mbabane
166	Sweden	Stockholm
167	Switzerland	Bern
168	Syria	Damascus
169	Taiwan	Taipei
170	Tajikistan	Dushanbe
171	Tanzania	Dar es Salaam
172	Thailand	Bangkok
173	Togo	Lomé
174	Tonga	Nuku'alofa
175	Trinidad & Tobago	Port-of-Spain
176	Tunisia	Tunis
177	Turkey	Ankara
178	Turkmenistan	Ashgabat
179	Tuvalu	Funafuti
180	Uganda	Kampala
181	Ukraine	Kiev
182	United Arab Emirates	Abu Dhabi
183	United Kingdom	London
184	United States	Washington
185	Uruguay	Montevideo
186	Uzbekistan	Tashkent
187	Vanuatu	Vila
188	Venezuela	Caracas
189	Vietnam	Hanoi
190	Western Sahara	El Aaiún
191	Yemen	Sana'a
192	Zaire	Kinshasa
193	Zambia	Lusaka
194	Zimbabwe	Harare

MARSHALL ISLANDS Majuro
KIRIBATI Tarawa
PAPUA NEW GUINEA Port Moresby
SOLOMON ISLANDS Honiara
TUVALU Funafuti
VANUATU Vila
FIJI Suva
SAMOA Apia
TONGA Nukualofa
AUSTRALIA Canberra
NEW ZEALAND Wellington

TAIWAN Taipei
VIETNAM Hanoi
LAOS Vientiane
BURMA Rangoon
THAILAND Bangkok
CAMBODIA Phnom Penh
PHILIPPINES Manila
MALAYSIA Kuala Lumpur
SINGAPORE Singapore
BRUNEI Bandar Seri Begawan
INDONESIA Jakarta
PALAU Koror

CHINA Beijing
NORTH KOREA P'yongyang
SOUTH KOREA Seoul
JAPAN Tokyo

MONGOLIA Ulaanbaatar
INDIA New Delhi
NEPAL Kathmandu
BHUTAN Thimphu
BANGLADESH Dhaka
SRI LANKA Colombo

UZBEKISTAN Tashkent
TAJIKISTAN Dushanbe
KYRGYZSTAN Bishkek
KAZAKHSTAN Astana
AFGHANISTAN Kabul
PAKISTAN Islamabad

TURKEY Ankara
CYPRUS Nicosia
LEBANON Beirut
SYRIA Damascus
IRAQ Baghdad
GEORGIA Tbilisi
ARMENIA Yerevan
AZERBAIJAN Baku
KUWAIT Kuwait
IRAN Tehran
BAHRAIN Manama
TURKMENISTAN Ashgabat

OMAN Muscat
UNITED ARAB EMIRATES Abu Dhabi
YEMEN Sana'a

MALDIVES Male
ERITREA Asmara
DJIBOUTI Djibouti
SUDAN Khartoum
ETHIOPIA Addis Ababa
SOMALIA Mogadishu
SEYCHELLES Victoria
THE COMOROS Moroni
MADAGASCAR Antananarivo
MAURITIUS Port Louis

TANZANIA Dar es Salaam
KENYA Nairobi
UGANDA Kampala
RWANDA Kigali
BURUNDI Bujumbura
MALAWI Lilongwe
ZAMBIA Lusaka
ZIMBABWE Harare
MOZAMBIQUE Maputo

MACEDONIA Skopje
BELARUS Minsk
BULGARIA Sofia
ROMANIA Bucharest
MOLDOVA Chisinau
UKRAINE Kiev
RUSSIA Moscow

FINLAND Helsinki
ESTONIA Tallinn
SWEDEN Stockholm
LATVIA Riga
NORWAY Oslo
LITHUANIA Vilnus

DENMARK Copenhagen
POLAND Warsaw
GERMANY Berlin
CZECH REPUBLIC Prague
NETHERLANDS Amsterdam
AUSTRIA Vienna
BELGIUM Brussels
LUXEMBOURG Luxembourg
SLOVAKIA Bratislava
HUNGARY Budapest
LIECHTENSTEIN Vaduz
SWITZERLAND Bern
SLOVENIA Ljubljana
CROATIA Zagreb
SERBIA Belgrade

BOSNIA & HERZEGOVINA Sarajevo
MONACO Monaco
HOLY SEE Vatican City
ITALY Rome
ALBANIA Tirane
GREECE Athens
TUNISIA Tunis
MALTA Valletta
LIBYA Tripoli

JORDAN Amman
ISRAEL Jerusalem
EGYPT Cairo
QATAR Doha
SAUDI ARABIA Riyadh

CHAD N'Djamena
NIGERIA Abuja
CAMEROON Yaounde
EQUATORIAL GUINEA Malabo
SAO TOME & PRINCIPE São Tomé

GABON Libreville
CENTRAL AFRICAN REPUBLIC Bangui
CONGO (REP OF) Brazzaville
CONGO (DEM REP OF) Kinshasa
ANGOLA Luanda

NAMIBIA Windhoek
BOTSWANA Gaborone
SOUTH AFRICA Pretoria
SWAZILAND Mbabane
LESOTHO Maseru

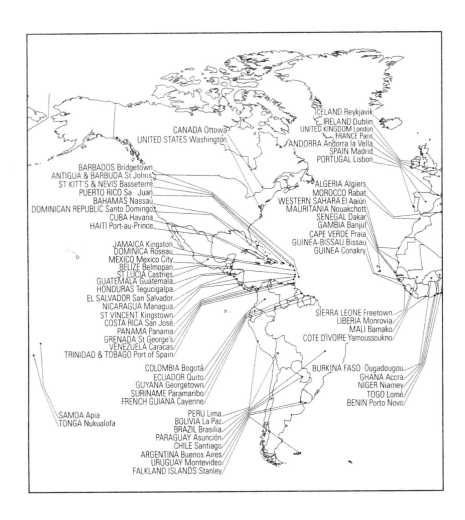

Kings and Queens
of England

For those who are in any way interested in the history of England, knowledge of the time-location and duration of reign provides an excellent matrix on which to 'hang' other knowledge matrices, including social, literary, religious, musical, artistic and scientific developments.

Onword

By this stage your skill with SEM^3 should have reached such a level that memorising this entire chunk of history (a task considered practically impossible by most history students) will take less than an hour!

		From	To
1	**William I**	1066	1087
2	**William II**	1087	1100
3	**Henry I**	1100	1135
4	**Stephen**	1135	1154
5	**Henry II**	1154	1189
6	**Richard I**	1189	1199
7	**John**	1199	1216
8	**Henry III**	1216	1272
9	**Edward I**	1272	1307

		From	To
10	Edward II	1307	1327
11	Edward III	1327	1377
12	Richard II	1377	1399
13	Henry IV	1399	1413
14	Henry V	1413	1422
15	Henry VI	1422	1461
16	Edward IV	1461	1483
17	Edward V	1483	1483
18	Richard III	1483	1485
19	Henry VII	1485	1509
20	Henry VIII	1509	1547
21	Edward VI	1547	1553
22	Jane	1553	1553
23	Mary I	1553	1558
24	Elizabeth I	1558	1603
25	James I	1603	1625
26	Charles I	1625	1649
27	Oliver Cromwell:		
	Lord Protector	1653	1658
28	Richard Cromwell:		
	Lord Protector	1658	1659
29	Charles II	1660	1685
30	James II	1685	1688
31	William III	1688	1702
32	and Mary II	1688	1694
33	Anne	1702	1714
34	George I	1714	1727
35	George II	1727	1760
36	George III	1760	1820
37	George IV	1820	1830
38	William IV	1830	1837
39	Victoria	1837	1901
40	Edward VII	1901	1910
41	George V	1910	1936
42	Edward VIII	1936	1936
43	George VI	1936	1952
44	Elizabeth II	1952	

The
Human Body –
Musculature

17

Memorising your own musculature gives you a more accurate understanding and appreciation of your own extraordinary complexity, allows you to train yourself with more precision and delicacy, to react more appropriately to any injury or medical condition, and to appreciate even more the accomplishments of those who have trained their own musculature to the level of championship performance.

Brain
Bites

Mental giants such as Michelangelo and Leonardo da Vinci spent years of their lives investigating the body's intricate interconnections and biophysical mechanics.

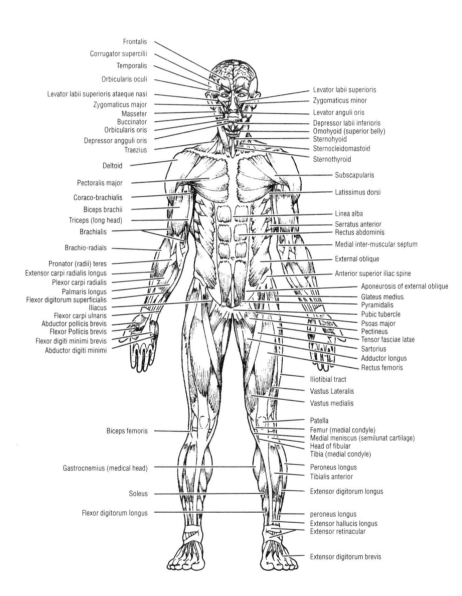

Frontalis
Corrugator supercilii
Temporalis
Orbicularis oculi
Levator labii superioris ataeque nasi
Zygomaticus major
Masseter
Buccinator
Orbicularis oris
Depressor angguli oris
Traezius
Deltoid
Pectoralis major
Coraco-brachialis
Biceps brachii
Triceps (long head)
Brachialis
Brachio-radials
Pronator (radii) teres
Extensor carpi radialis longus
Plexor carpi radialis
Palmaris longus
Flexor digitorum superficialis
Iliacus
Flexor carpi ulnaris
Abductor pollicis brevis
Flexor Pollicis brevis
Flexor digiti minimi brevis
Abductor digiti minimi

Biceps femoris

Gastrocnemius (medical head)

Soleus

Flexor digitorum longus

Levator labii superioris
Zygomaticus minor
Levator anguli oris
Depressor labii inferioris
Omohyoid (superior belly)
Sternohyoid
Sternocleidomastoid
Sternothyroid
Subscapularis
Latissimus dorsi
Linea alba
Serratus anterior
Rectus abdominis
Medial inter-muscular septum
External oblique
Anterior superior iliac spine
Aponeurosis of external oblique
Glateus medius
Pyramidalis
Pubic tubercle
Psoas major
Pectineus
Tensor fasciae latae
Sartorius
Adductor longus
Rectus femoris
Iliotibial tract
Vastus Lateralis
Vastus medialis
Patella
Femur (medial condyle)
Medial meniscus (semilunat cartilage)
Head of fibular
Tibia (medial condyle)
Peroneus longus
Tibialis anterior
Extensor digitorum longus
peroneus longus
Extensor hallucis longus
Extensor retinacular
Extensor digitorum brevis

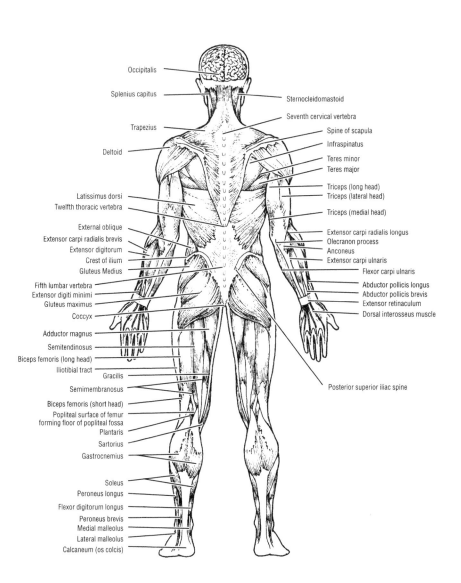

Occipitalis

Splenius capitus

Trapezius

Deltoid

Latissimus dorsi

Twelfth thoracic vertebra

External oblique

Extensor carpi radialis brevis

Extensor digitorum

Crest of ilium

Gluteus Medius

Fifth lumbar vertebra

Extensor digiti minimi

Gluteus maximus

Coccyx

Adductor magnus

Semitendinosus

Biceps femoris (long head)

Iliotibial tract

Gracilis

Semimembranosus

Biceps femoris (short head)

Popliteal surface of femur
forming floor of popliteal fossa

Plantaris

Sartorius

Gastrocnemius

Soleus

Peroneus longus

Flexor digitorum longus

Peroneus brevis

Medial malleolus

Lateral malleolus

Calcaneum (os colcis)

Sternocleidomastoid

Seventh cervical vertebra

Spine of scapula

Infraspinatus

Teres minor

Teres major

Triceps (long head)

Triceps (lateral head)

Triceps (medial head)

Extensor carpi radialis longus

Olecranon process

Anconeus

Extensor carpi ulnaris

Flexor carpi ulnaris

Abductor pollicis longus

Abductor pollicis brevis

Extensor retinaculum

Dorsal interosseus muscle

Posterior superior iliac spine

You would apply SEM^3 to the memorisation of the body's musculature (pages 164–5) in the following way: suppose, for example, the first item you want to memorise is the first muscle on the head, i.e. the *Frontalis*. This you will place as number '1' on the Major System – *day*. What does *Frontalis* sound like? How about the 'front of Alice'? You could choose an Alice you know, or, perhaps more preferably, Alice in Wonderland. You might visualise her vividly in a blue dress and white apron with beautiful long, wavy, golden hair. Let's put this information under the Rainbow section of SEM^3 and use the colour yellow. Imagine it's the beginning of another wonderful day – a glorious yellow dawn, and over the horizon, instead of the sun, comes Alice! From her *Frontalis* area comes a dazzling yellow light, which suffuses the whole sky, while the rest of Alice gradually rises over the horizon, as the blazing yellow light becomes stronger and stronger. If you have visualised this image well, you will remember where the *Frontalis* area is for the rest of your life.

Let's try one more: *Orbicularis oculi*. This sounds a bit like 'orbit-cular' (an ancient Roman god of the household) -es (the plural of 'lar' is 'lares' -o-culi. Noah's Ark is your number '2'. Paint it a vivid yellow, and on the side of it, painted a darker yellow, is a section of the face that includes the *Orbicularis oculi*. Your special ark, however, is going to go up in *orbit!* In the *cu* of animals are some rather odd-looking characters: twins of the Roman god *lar* (*lares*) and in the middle of them is *oculi*. Easy, isn't it?

The 18 Elements

Our selves, our planet, our solar system and indeed our universe are made up primarily of 105 elements or 'basic working parts'.

Thus the vast majesty of the microcosmos and macrocosmos that surrounds us can, like a language, have its astounding complexity reduced to fundamental operating parts that allow us to understand and learn about it with much greater facility.

Once you have control of these, and the way in which they fit together, your ability to create understanding and inter-relationships and 'structures' within the field becomes limitless.

Using SEM^3, you will be able to lay a complete foundation for your growing understanding of the physical, chemical and biological worlds around you – a level of understanding that most people never attain, even after four years of study.

You will also be laying the cornerstones for answering those probing questions that children ask in order to understand the world around them: 'Why does water go hard when it's cold?'; 'Why do things smell and taste different?'; 'Why do sugar and salt taste different although they look the same?'; 'Why do I have to eat?!'

As SEM^3 is a Master Matrix that allows you to structure your memory, so the Matrix of the chemical elements is a Master Matrix that allows you to understand the structure and nature of the physical universe.

The names of the various families or groupings of the elements are as follows:

Hydrogen
Noble Gases
Alkali and Alkaline Earth Metals   (abb. Alkaline)
Boron and Carbon Families   (abb. Boron/Carbon)
Nitrogen and Oxygen Families   (abb. Nitrogen/Oxygen)
The Halogens
Early Transition Metals   (abb. Early Trans Metals)
Late Transition Metals   (abb. Late Trans Metals)
The Triads
Rare Earth Metals
Actinide Metals   (abb. Actinide)

Atomic Number	Elements	Symbol	Atomic Weight	Family
1	HYDROGEN	H	1.008	HYDROGEN

From hydro and gen, or water-forming; discovered in 1766; third most abundant and lightest element. Hydrogen is almost never found free on earth, but the sun and other stars are almost pure hydrogen. The thermonuclear fusion of hydrogen nuclei lights and heats the universe.

| 2 | HELIUM | He | 4.0026 | NOBLE GASES |

From helios, or sun; discovered in 1868; almost all the helium in the world comes from natural gas wells in the United States. One well in Arizona produces a gas that is 8% helium. Lighter than air, it is widely used in balloons in place of highly inflammable hydrogen.

| 3 | LITHIUM | Li | 6.941 | ALKALINE |

From lithos; discovered in 1817; the lightest of the solid elements. Lithium forms a black oxide when exposed to air. It is used in ceramics, alloys, in the H-bomb – and in treating both gout victims and manic-depressives.

| 4 | BERYLLIUM | Be | 9.012 | ALKALINE |

From the mineral beryl, in which it was found in 1798. This element produces alloys that are extremely elastic, hence its role in making gears, springs and other machine parts. Because of its high melting point – 1285°C – beryllium is used in making rocket nose cones.

| 5 | BORON | B | 10.811 | BORON/CARBON |

From borax and carbon; discovered 1808. A non-metal, boron is best known in borax (sodium borate) and in boric-acid – the one acid that is good for the eyes. About a million tons of boron are used in industry each year. In agriculture it serves as both a plant food and a weed killer.

Atomic Number	Elements	Symbol	Atomic Weight	Family
6	CARBON	C	12.011	BORON/CARBON

From carbo, or charcoal; prehistoric. Carbon, in its endless variety of compounds, is an indispensable source of everyday products, such as nylon and petrol, perfume and plastics, shoe polish, DDT and TNT.

7	NITROGEN	N	14.007	NITROGEN/OXYGEN

From nitron and gen, or nitre-forming; discovered in 1772; a gas making up 78% of the air. Nitrogen can be 'fixed' from the air – compounds include the anaesthetic 'laughing gas', explosives such as TNT, fertilisers and amino acids – the building blocks of protein.

8	OXYGEN	O	15.999	NITROGEN/OXYGEN

From oxys and gen, or acid-forming; discovered in 1774; the most abundant element, making up about half of everything on earth, 21% of the atmosphere by volume and two-thirds of the human body. Breathed in by animals, oxygen is restored to the air by plants.

9	FLUORINE	F	18.998	HALOGENS

From fluor, or flow; discovered in 1771. Fluorine is the most reactive of the non-metals; only a few of the inert gases resist it. It corrodes platinum, a material that withstands most other chemicals. In a stream of fluorine gas, wood and rubber burst into flame – and even asbestos glows.

10	NEON	Ne	20.183	NOBLE GASES

From neos, or new; discovered 1898. The best known of the inert gases, it is chiefly used in advertising. The ubiquitous 'neon sign' is a glass vacuum tube containing a minute amount of neon gas; when an electric current is passed through, the tube gives off a bright orange-red light.

11	SODIUM	Na	22.990	ALKALINE

From soda; symbol from its Latin name Natrium; discovered 1807; sixth most abundant element. Metallic sodium is too violent for most everyday uses and is generally stored in paraffin. But its useful compounds include table salt, baking soda, borax and lye.

12	MAGNESIUM	Mg	24.3	ALKALINE

From Magnesia, an ancient city in Asia Minor; discovered 1775; eighth most abundant element; burns as a powder or foil in firecrackers, bombs and flash bulbs. It has one odd biological effect: a deficiency in man can have the same effect as alcoholism, delirium tremens.

13	ALUMINIUM	Al	26.982	BORON/CARBON

From alumen, or alum; discovered 1827; the most abundant metal and third most abundant element, its uses range from toothpaste tubes to aeroplane wings. Early samples cost £230 per pound; over a million tons are produced yearly in the US for as little as 30 pence per pound.

Atomic Number	Elements	Symbol	Atomic Weight	Family
14	SILICON	Si	28.086	BORON/CARBON

From silex, or flint; discovered 1823; the second most abundant element – making up one-quarter of the earth's crust. Sand, largely silicon dioxide, goes into making glass and cement. Pure silicon is used in micro-electronic devices such as solar batteries to power satellite instruments.

15	PHOSPHORUS	P	30.974	NITROGEN/OXYGEN

From phosphoros, or light bearer; discovered 1669; occurs in three major forms – white, red and rarely black. The white is so unstable that it yellows then reddens in light, glows in the dark – hence 'phosphorescence'. Phosphates are ingredients of detergents.

16	SULPHUR	S	32.064	NITROGEN/OXYGEN

From sulphur (or brimstone, its biblical name); recognised since ancient times. Used in all branches of modern industry, it is found in matches, insecticides and rubber tyres. Nearly 200 pounds of sulphuric acid per capita are produced in the US each year.

17	CHLORINE	Cl	35.453	HALOGENS

From chloros, or greenish-yellow; discovered 1774. Combining with almost as many elements as fluorine, chlorine is less corrosive but strong enough to be used as a bleach, a disinfectant and a poison gas. Pure chlorine is commonly prepared from ordinary salt.

18	ARGON	Ar	39.948	NOBLE GASES

From argon, or inactive; discovered 1894. The most abundant of noble gases, argon makes up 0.934% of the air. Its industrial forte is in welding; it provides an inert atmosphere in which welded metals will not burn. It is also the gas that fills ordinary incandescent light bulbs.

19	POTASSIUM	K	39.1	ALKALINE

From potash, an impure form of potassium carbonate known to the ancients; symbol K from its Latin name kalium; discovered 1807. Seventh most abundant element in the earth's crust. Its radioactivity, though mild, may be one natural cause of genetic mutation in man.

20	CALCIUM	Ca	40.08	ALKALINE

From calx, or lime – an oxide of calcium; discovered 1808; fifth most abundant element in the earth's crust. Its presence in our bodies is essential. Normal quota in an adult is about 2 pounds, mostly in the teeth and bones. Calcium also plays a role in regulating the heartbeat.

21	SCANDIUM	SC	44.956	EARLY TRANS METALS

From Scandinavia; discovered 1879. Although no practical uses have yet been found for this metal, its potential is great because it is almost as light as aluminium and has a much higher melting point. A pound of scandium produced in 1960 was the first such quantity

Atomic Number	Elements	Symbol	Atomic Weight	Family
22	TITANIUM	Ti	47.9	EARLY TRANS METALS

From Titans, the supermen of Greek myth; discovered in 1791. Although it is the ninth most abundant element, titanium has only recently begun to serve man. Its white dioxide goes into bright paints. The metal itself is used in constructing supersonic aircraft such as Concorde.

23	VANADIUM	V	50.942	EARLY TRANS METALS

From Vanadis, a Scandinavian goddess; discovered 1830. Added to steel, vanadium produces one of the toughest alloys for armour plate, axles, piston rods and crankshafts. Less than 1% of vanadium and a little chromium makes steel shock- and vibration-resistant.

24	CHROMIUM	Cr	51.996	EARLY TRANS METALS

From chroma, or colour; discovered 1797. A very bright silvery metal, it forms compounds valued as pigments for their vivid green, yellow, red and orange colours. The ruby takes its colour from chromium. Besides lustrous chrome plate, its alloys include a number of special hard steels.

25	MANGANESE	Mn	54.938	EARLY TRANS METALS

From magnes, or magnet – its ore was first confused with magnetic iron ore; discovered 1774. Manganese, which gives steel a hard yet pliant quality, seems to play a similar role in animal bone: without it, bones grow spongier and break more easily. It activates many enzymes.

26	IRON	Fe	55.847	TRIADS

From iren, its old English name; symbol Fe from its Latin name, ferrum; first utilised by prehistoric man. The fourth most abundant element and the cheapest metal, iron is the basic ingredient of all steel. Making up part of the compound haemoglobin, it carries oxygen in the bloodstream.

27	COBALT	Co	58.933	TRIADS

From kobold, or evil spirit (its poisonous ores were once treacherous to mine); discovered 1735. For centuries cobalt's blue salts have given colour to porcelains, tiles and enamels. Its alloys go into making jet propulsion engines, and its radioactive isotope is used to treat cancer.

28	NICKEL	Ni	58.7	TRIADS

From the German Kupfernickel, or false copper, a reddish ore contains nickel but no copper; discovered 1751. Its hard durable qualities have long made nickel popular for coins – the US 5-cent piece is 25% nickel, the rest copper. Nickel plate protects softer metals.

29	COPPER	Cu	63.5	LATE TRANS METALS

From cuprum, derived from the ancient name of Cyprus, famed for its copper mines; known by early man. It and gold are the only two coloured metals. Alloyed in most gold jewellery and silverware, copper is mixed with zinc in brass, with tin in bronze. A 'copper' penny is bronze.

Atomic Number	Elements	Symbol	Atomic Weight	Family
30	ZINC	Zn	65.38	LATE TRANS METALS

Probably from zin, German for tin; discovered by the alchemist Paracelsus in the sixteenth century, though the zinc-copper alloy brass was known to the ancients. While not technically a coloured metal, zinc has a bluish cast. An excellent coating metal, it is used to line flashlight batteries.

31	GALLIUM	Ga	69.72	BORON/CARBON

From Gallia, the old name for France; discovered 1875. A metal that melts in the hand, it is one of the few that expands as it freezes, as do non-metals and most gases. Its high boiling point – 1983°C – makes it ideal for recording temperatures that would vaporise a thermometer.

32	GERMANIUM	Ge	72.59	BORON/CARBON

From Germany; discovered 1886. The first metal in the carbon family, germanium resembles the non-metal silicon. The first element used for transistors, it has brought about the replacement of large vacuum tubes with devices $1/400$ inch across.

33	ARSENIC	As	74.933	NITROGEN/OXYGEN

From arsenikos, or male (the Greeks believed metals differed in sex); discovered about 1250. Best classed as a non-metal with a few metallic traits, arsenic is famed as a poison but some of its compounds are medicines. When heated it 'sublimes' – i.e the solid evaporates directly.

34	SELENIUM	Se	78.96	NITROGEN/OXYGEN

From selene, or moon; discovered 1817; exists both as metal and non-metal. Unlike most electrical conductors, selenium varies in conductivity with variations in light. This 'photo-electric' trait makes it suitable for use in electric eyes, solar cells, television cameras and light meters.

35	BROMINE	Br	79.9	HALOGENS

From bromos, or stench; discovered 1826; a red, caustic, fuming liquid, with a foul smell. Bromine is an effective disinfectant. Among its compounds are the bromides, used in nerve sedatives, and in petrol anti-knock compounds that make car engines run smoothly.

36	KRYPTON	Kr	83.8	NOBLE GASES

From kryptos, or hidden; discovered in 1898. Radioactive krypton is used to keep tabs on Soviet nuclear production. Because this gas is a by-product of all nuclear reactors, the Russian share is found by subtracting the amount that comes from Western reactors from the total in the air.

37	RUBIDIUM	Rb	85.47	ALKALINE

From rubidus, or red (the colour its salts impart to flames); discovered 1861. Used in electric eye-cells, also a potential space fuel. Like potassium, it is slightly radioactive, and has been used to locate brain tumours, as it collects in tumours but not in normal tissue.

Atomic Number	Elements	Symbol	Atomic Weight	Family
38	STRONTIUM	Sr	87.62	ALKALINE

From Strontian, Scotland; discovered 1790; a rare metal which is a sort of evil alter ego of life-supporting calcium. Radioactive strontium 90 is present in atomic fall-out. It is absorbed by bone tissue in place of calcium; enough of it destroys marrow and can cause cancer.

39	YTTRIUM	Y	88.9	EARLY TRANS METALS

From the town of Ytterby, Sweden, where it was discovered in 1794; a scaly metal with an iron-grey sheen. Yttrium 90, a radioactive isotope, has a dramatic medical use in needles which have replaced the surgeon's knife in killing pain-transmitting nerves in the spinal cord.

40	ZIRCONIUM	Zr	91.22	EARLY TRANS METALS

From zircon, the name of the semi-precious gemstone in which it was discovered in 1789. A metal unaffected by neutrons, zirconium serves as the inner lining of reactors in nuclear submarines and atomic power plants. It is also used as a building material for jets and rockets.

41	NIOBIUM	Nb	92.906	EARLY TRANS METALS

From Niobe, daughter of the mythical Greek king Tantalus (niobium is found with tantalum); discovered 1801. Used in steel, atomic reactors, jet engines and rockets, it was known until 1950 as colombium, from Columbus – a poetic name for America, where its ore was first discovered.

42	MOLYBDENUM	Mo	95.94	EARLY TRANS METALS

From molybdos, or lead – first found in what was originally thought to be lead-ore; discovered 1778. Fifth highest melting metal, it is used in boiler plate, rifle barrels and filaments. No vessel could be found in which to cast it until a special water-cooled crucible was devised in 1959.

43	TECHNETIUM	Tc	98	EARLY TRANS METALS

From technetos, or artificial; produced 1937. The first man-made element, it was originally produced by the atomic bombardment of molybdenum. Later it was found among the fission products of uranium

44	RUTHENIUM	Ru	101.07	THE TRIADS

From Ruthenia, Latin for Russia; discovered 1844. Pure ruthenium is too hard and brittle to machine. It makes an excellent 'hardener', however, when it is alloyed with platinum. But used in excess of 15%, ruthenium is ruinous, making the metals too hard to be worked.

45	RHODIUM	Rh	102.91	THE TRIADS

From rhodon, or rose (its salts give a rosy solution); discovered 1803. Besides forming alloys, rhodium makes a lustrous, hard coating for other metals in such items as table silver and camera parts. A thin film of vaporised rhodium deposited on glass makes a very good mirror.

Atomic Number	Elements	Symbol	Atomic Weight	Family
46	PALLADIUM	Pd	106.4	THE TRIADS

After the asteroid Pallas; discovered 1803. Free from tarnish and corrosion-resistant, palladium is incorporated in contacts for telephone relays and high-grade surgical instruments. It is also used with gold, silver and other metals as a 'stiffener' in dental inlays and bridgework.

47	SILVER	Ag	107.87	LATE TRANS METALS

From Old English seolfor, for silver; symbol Ag from its Latin name argentum; prehistoric; the best conductor of heat and electricity. Its salts are basic in photography; when silver bromide is exposed to light, it undergoes a chemical change which the developer then makes visible.

48	CADMIUM	Cd	112.4	LATE TRANS METALS

From kadmia, or earth; discovered 1817. Cadmium occurs in nature with zinc. It makes excellent neutron-eating rods to slow down atomic chain reactions and finds use in nickel-cadmium batteries. Its bright sulphide makes the popular artist's pigment, cadmium yellow.

49	INDIUM	In	114.82	BORON/CARBON

From the indigo blue it shows in a spectroscope; discovered 1863. A metal used in engine bearings, in transistors and as a 'glue' that adheres to glass, it is too scarce for large-scale use. But a minuscule, long-lived indium battery has been devised to power electronic wrist watches.

50	TIN	Sn	118.69	BORON/CARBON

An Old English word; symbol Sn from stannum, Latin for tin. Prehistoric. Because it does not rust and resists other corrosion, tin has made canned food possible. A tin can is steel-coated with about 0.0005 of an inch of tin. Over 40,000 million cans are made each year.

51	ANTIMONY	Sb	121.75	NITROGEN/OXYGEN

From antimonas, 'opposed to solitude' (it generally occurs mixed with other elements); symbol Sb from stibium, or mark (it was once used as eyebrow pencil). Discovered about 1450. Antimony is mixed with lead in batteries and goes into type metal and pewter alloys.

52	TELLURIUM	Te	127.60	NITROGEN/OXYGEN

From tellus, the earth; discovered 1782. With both metallic and non-metallic traits, tellurium has several peculiarities. It is 'out of step' in the periodic table, having a lower atomic number but higher atomic weight than iodine. And inhaling its vapour results in garlicky breath.

53	IODINE	I	126.90	THE HALOGENS

From iodes, or violet; discovered 1811. A blue-black solid which turns into a violet vapour when heated. Formerly prepared from seaweed, it is now produced from oil-well brines. Most table salt is now 'iodised' to supplement the human diet; an iodine deficiency causes thyroid trouble.

Atomic Number	Elements	Symbol	Atomic Weight	Family
54	XENON	Xe	131.3	NOBLE GASES

From xenos, or stranger; discovered 1898. The rarest gas in the atmosphere, xenon is used in specialised light sources such as the high-speed electronic flash bulbs used by photographers. In these, the high volatility of its electron structure produces an instant, intense light.

55	CAESIUM	Cs	132.91	ALKALINE

From caesius, or sky-blue (its salts turn flames blue); discovered 1860; the softest metal, liquid at warm room temperature, 28°C. Extremely reactive, it finds limited use in vacuum tubes and in atomic clocks so accurate that they vary no more than five seconds in ten generations.

56	BARIUM	Ba	137.3	ALKALINE

From barys, heavy or dense; discovered 1808. The white sulphate is drunk as a medical cocktail to outline the stomach and intestines for X-ray examination. Barium nitrate gives fireworks a green colour.

57	LANTHANUM	La	138.91	EARLY TRANS METALS

From lanthanein, to lie hidden; discovered 1839; highly reactive. Because it gives glass special light-bending, or 'refractive', properties, lanthanum is used in expensive camera lenses. Radioactive lanthanum has been tested for use in treating cancer.

58	CERIUM	Ce	140.12	RARE EARTH METALS

After the asteroid Ceres; discovered 1803; most abundant of the rare-earth elements. It is the chief ingredient (just under 50%) of misch-metal alloy. Cerium is used in alloys to make heat-resistant jet-engine parts; its oxide is a promising new petroleum-cracking catalyst.

59	PRASEODYMIUM	Pr	140.91	RARE EARTH METALS

From prasios didymos, or green twin (from its green salts); discovered 1885 when separated from its rare-earth twin neodymium. Together they are now used in making lenses for glassmaker's goggles because they filter out the yellow light present in glass blowing.

60	NEODYMIUM	Nd	144.24	RARE EARTH METALS

From neos didymium, or new twin; discovered 1885. In a pure form, it produces the only bright-purple glass known. In a cruder state, it is used to take colour out of glass and to make special glass that transmits the tanning rays of the sun but not the unwanted infra-red heat rays.

61	PROMETHIUM	Pm	145	RARE EARTH METALS

After Prometheus; discovered 1947; the only rare earth that has never been found in nature. Produced in nuclear reactors, radioactive promethium in an 'atomic battery' no bigger than a drawing pin powers guided-missile instruments, watches and radios.

Atomic Number	Elements	Symbol	Atomic Weight	Family
62	SAMARIUM	Sm	150.36	RARE EARTH METALS

From the mineral samarskite, named after a Russian mine official, Colonel V.E. Samarsky; discovered 1879. Calcium chloride crystals treated with samarium have been employed in lasers – devices for producing beams of light intense enough to burn metal or bounce off the moon.

63	EUROPIUM	Eu	151.96	RARE EARTH METALS

From Europe; discovered 1896. Most reactive rare earth. The metal had virtually no practical use until the atomic age. But atom for atom, europium can absorb more neutrons than any other element, making it valuable in control rods for nuclear reactors.

64	GADOLINIUM	Gd	157.25	RARE EARTH METALS

From the mineral gadolinite, named after a Finnish chemist; discovered 1880. Falling in the middle of the rare-earth series, gadolinium divides the lighter metals, which tend to impart pliant qualities to alloys, from the heavier metals, used mostly as strengthening agents.

65	TERBIUM	Tb	158.9	RARE EARTH METALS

From Ytterby, Sweden; discovered 1843; named after the town that also gave its name to three other elements; the rare earths ytterbium and erbium and the transition metal yttrium. Like all rare earths, terbium in an impure state is pyrophoric – i.e. it bursts into flame when heated.

66	DYSPROSIUM	Dy	162.50	RARE EARTH METALS

From dysprositos, or hard to get at; discovered 1886. Dysprosium's chief practical use is in nuclear reactors, where it serves as a nuclear 'poison' – i.e. it is employed as a neutron-eating material to keep the neutron-spawning atomic chain reaction from getting out of hand.

67	HOLMIUM	Ho	164.93	RARE EARTH METALS

From Holmia, Latin name for Stockholm; discovered 1879. Like dysprosium, holmium is a metal which can absorb fission-bred neutrons. It is used in nuclear reactors as a burnable poison – i.e. one that burns up while it is keeping a chain reaction from running out of control.

68	ERBIUM	Er	167.26	RARE EARTH METALS

From Ytterby, Sweden; discovered 1843. Used in ceramics as erbium oxide to produce a pink glaze. Erbium, holmium and dysprosium are almost identical in terms of their chemical and physical properties. They vary from each other only by one electron in their third inner orbit.

69	THULIUM	Tm	168.93	RARE EARTH METALS

From Thule, or Northland; discovered 1879. When irradiated in a nuclear reactor, thulium produces an isotope that gives off X-rays. A 'button' of this isotope is used to make a lightweight, portable X-ray machine for medical use. The 'hot' thulium is replaced every few months.

Atomic Number	Elements	Symbol	Atomic Weight	Family
70	YTTERBIUM	Yb	173.04	RARE EARTH METALS

From Ytterby, Sweden; discovered 1907. This element is still little more than a laboratory curiosity. Along with the other rare earths, it recently turned up in Russia in a mineral called gagarinite after the first astronaut. Easily oxidised.

71	LUTETIUM	Lu	174.97	RARE EARTH METALS

From Lutetia, the ancient name for Paris; discovered 1907; heaviest of the rare earths. Although rare-earth alloys such as misch metal are cheap, pure lutetium is highly expensive. With many of its chemical and physical properties unknown, it has no practical value.

72	HAFNIUM	Hf	178.49	EARLY TRANS METALS

From Hafnia, the Latin name for Copenhagen; discovered 1923. A 'wonder metal' of the atomic age, hafnium has a great appetite for neutrons. Thus it goes into neutron-absorbing reactor control rods which slow down nuclear chain reactions and also quench atomic 'fires'.

73	TANTALUM	Ta	180.95	EARLY TRANS METALS

From King Tantalus of Greek myth; discovered 1802. Almost impervious to corrosion, tantalum is vital in surgical repairs of the human body; it can replace bone (for example in skull plates); as foil or wire it connects torn nerves; as woven gauze it binds up abdominal muscles.

74	TUNGSTEN	W	183.85	EARLY TRANS METALS

From Swedish tungsten, or heavy stone; symbol W from its German name wolfram; discovered 1783. The highest melting of metals at 3410°C – tungsten in filaments withstands intense heat in light bulbs. New tungsten-tipped 'painless' dental drills spin at ultra-high speed.

75	RHENIUM	Re	186.2	EARLY TRANS METALS

From the Rhine provinces of Germany; discovered 1925. Rhenium is the ninth scarcest element and has the second highest melting point. It is used in 'thermocouples' (electric thermometers for measuring high temperatures) and in the contact points of electrical switches.

76	OSMIUM	Os	190.2	THE TRIADS

From osme, or odour; discovered 1804. A metal with a pungent smell, it is used to produce alloys of extreme hardness. Pen tips and 'lifetime' gramophone needles are 60% osmium. It is the densest metal known: a brick-sized chunk of osmium weighs about 56 pounds.

77	IRIDIUM	Ir	192.2	THE TRIADS

From iris, or rainbow, so named for its colourful salts; discovered 1804. Very hard and hence extremely difficult to work, iridium hardens other metals. Its alloys make bars used as standard weights and measures. The international 'standard metre' is platinum-iridium.

Atomic Number	Elements	Symbol	Atomic Weight	Family
78	PLATINUM	Pt	195.08	THE TRIADS

From platina, or little silver; discovered in the sixteenth century. Found in nuggets of up to 21 pounds, it is used not only in weights and measures but also in catalysts, delicate instruments and electrical equipment. Its cost (more than gold) has demanded a hallmark for platinum jewellery.

79	GOLD	Au	196.97	LATE TRANS METALS

From the Old English word geolo, or yellow; symbol Au from its Latin name aurum; prehistoric; the most malleable metal. Man's lust for gold has been a delusion, for he has pursued little more than a yellow gleam. Until the advent of computer components, it could not be used for much besides money, jewellery and dental work.

80	MERCURY	Hg	200.59	LATE TRANS METALS

From the planet Mercury; symbol Hg from hydrargyrum, or liquid silver; prehistoric. It appears in the glass tubing of thermometers and barometers; it also finds use in 'silver' dental inlays and in silent electric switches. Vaporised mercury fills modern blue-hued street lights.

81	THALLIUM	Tl	204.38	BORON/CARBON

From thallos, or a young shoot – its spectrum is a bright-green line; discovered 1861. Its chief use is in thallium sulphate – a deadly rat poison. Odourless and tasteless, it is mixed with starch, sugar, glycerine and water to make an inviting if ominous 'treat' for household rodents.

82	LEAD	Pb	207.2	BORON/CARBON

From Old English lead; symbol Pb from its Latin name, plumbum, also the origin of plumber. Prehistoric. Enormously durable, lead has been the backbone of plumbing for centuries. Lead pipes once used to drain the baths of ancient Rome have been uncovered still in working order.

83	BISMUTH	Bi	208.98	NITROGEN/OXYGEN

From the German wismuth, or white mass; discovered 1450. The most metallic member of its family, bismuth melts at 271°C but forms alloys that melt at as low as 47°C. These find wide application in electric fuses, solders and in automatic fire-sprinkler systems.

84	POLONIUM	Po	209	NITROGEN/OXYGEN

After Poland; found in 1898 by Pierre and Marie Curie in pitchblende. The scarcest natural element, it was the first to be discovered by the Curies. It is sold as an alpha-particle source for scientific use.

85	ASTATINE	At	210	THE HALOGENS

From astatos, or unstable; discovered 1940. Astatine, prepared by bombarding bismuth atoms with helium nuclei, is radioactive and has a maximum half-life of 83 hours. Its detection is recorded in the notebook of one of its discoverers, American physicist D.R. Corson.

Atomic Number	Elements	Symbol	Atomic Weight	Family
86	RADON	Rn	222	NOBLE GASES

From radium; discovered 1900. Heaviest gaseous element, it is emitted by radium and is itself radioactive; it decays into radioactive polonium and alpha rays. This radiation makes radon useful in cancer therapy; gold needles filled with the gas are implanted into the diseased tissue.

Atomic Number	Elements	Symbol	Atomic Weight	Family
87	FRANCIUM	Fr	223	ALKALINE

From France; discovered 1939. A short-lived product of the decay of actinium, francium has never actually been seen. A graph identifies francium by its radiation in the notebook of its discoverer, Marguerite Perey, a one-time assistant to Marie Curie.

Atomic Number	Elements	Symbol	Atomic Weight	Family
88	RADIUM	Ra	226	ALKALINE

From radius, or ray; discovered 1898 by Pierre and Marie Curie; sixth rarest of the elements. Radium bromide mixed with zinc sulphide is used in luminous watch dials. The radium gives off dangerous radiation which causes the zinc sulphide to glow.

Atomic Number	Elements	Symbol	Atomic Weight	Family
89	ACTINIUM	Ac	227	ACTINIDE

From aktinos, or ray; discovered 1899. Second rarest of the elements. Found in pitchblende. With a half-life of 22 years, actinium decomposes into francium and helium.

Atomic Number	Elements	Symbol	Atomic Weight	Family
90	THORIUM	Th	232.04	ACTINIDE

From Thor, Scandinavian war god; discovered 1828. Thorium can be used instead of scarce uranium as a reactor fuel because it is readily converted into uranium. Almost as abundant as lead, earthly thorium stores more energy than all uranium, coal, oil and other fuels combined.

Atomic Number	Elements	Symbol	Atomic Weight	Family
91	PROTACTINIUM	Pa	231	ACTINIDE

From protos, or first; it is the parent of actinium, which is formed by its radioactive decay; discovered 1917. Third rarest of the elements, it can be prepared by modern chemical techniques from thorium or uranium.

Atomic Number	Elements	Symbol	Atomic Weight	Family
92	URANIUM	U	238.03	ACTINIDE

After the planet Uranus; discovered 1789; the heaviest atom among the natural elements. Its most common form has a half-life of 4500 million years. In a nuclear reactor, it generates neutrons to keep the chain reaction going.

Atomic Number	Elements	Symbol	Atomic Weight	Family
93	NEPTUNIUM	Np	237	ACTINIDE

After Neptune, the planet beyond Uranus; discovered 1940. Detected first in invisible, unweighable amounts, neptunium was the first 'synthetic' element made from uranium. Traces of it turn up in uranium ores, produced by stray neutrons from uranium's decay.

Atomic Number	Elements	Symbol	Atomic Weight	Family
94	PLUTONIUM	Pu	244	ACTINIDE

After Pluto, the planet beyond Neptune; discovered 1940. Plutonium was used, instead of uranium, in several of the first atomic bombs. In one of the codes of wartime physicists, plutonium was referred to as 'copper'; copper itself had to be renamed 'honest-to-God copper'.

95	AMERICIUM	Am	243	ACTINIDE

Named after the Americas, by analogy with the rare earth europium; discovered 1944. Americium is produced by bombarding plutonium with neutrons. It has been made in gramme quantities which, in the world of such elements, is virtually a superabundance.

96	CURIUM	Cm	247	ACTINIDE

In honour of Pierre and Marie Curie, pioneers in the field of radioactivity; discovered 1944. Curium, with a half-life of 19 years, is a decay product of americium. Curium hydroxide is the first known curium compound.

97	BERKELIUM	Bk	247	ACTINIDE

After Berkeley, the home of the University of California, whose scientists have detected all 11 of the transuranium elements; discovered 1949. Many infinitesimal samples of berkelium have been prepared.

98	CALIFORNIUM	Cf	251	ACTINIDE

After the State and University of California; discovered 1950. Not until 1960 did californium exist in visible amounts.

99	EINSTEINIUM	Es	252	ACTINIDE

After Albert Einstein; discovered 1952. It was first detected in the debris from the 1952 H-bomb explosion at Eniwetok in the Pacific after tons of radioactive coral from atolls in the blast area were sifted and examined. The element was later made in a nuclear reactor.

100	FERMIUM	Fm	257	ACTINIDE

After Enrico Fermi; discovered 1953. Ferminium, like einsteinium, was first isolated from the debris of the 1952 H-bomb test, having been produced from the fission of uranium. Because of its short lifespan, scientists doubt that enough fermium will ever be obtained to be weighed.

101	MENDELEVIUM	Md	258	ACTINIDE

After Dmitri Mendeleyev, who devised the periodic table; discovered in 1955. Bombarding the scantest unweighable quantities of einsteinium with helium nuclei, scientists identified mendelevium from the barest shred of evidence – one to three atoms per bombardment.

102	NOBELIUM	No	259	ACTINIDE

After Alfred Nobel. A 1957 claim of discovery is disputed, but nobelium was positively identified in 1958 by a team of University of California scientists. Observations were not made on nobelium itself but on atoms of fermium 250 – 'daughter atoms' produced by nobelium's decay.

Atomic Number	Elements	Symbol	Atomic Weight	Family
103	LAWRENCIUM	Lr	260	ACTINIDE

After Ernest O Lawrence. Discovered in 1961 at Lawrence Radiation Laboratories, lawrencium was made by bombardment of californium with boron in a chamber fitted with a copper conveyor; the new atoms, one at a time, were carried to a radiation detector for identification.

Atomic Number	Elements	Symbol	Atomic Weight	Family
104	UNNILQUADIUM	Unq	261	ACTINIDE

Originally named after Lord Ernest Rutherford, was produced in 1969 at Lawrence Radiation Laboratory by bombardment of californium with carbon nuclei. Soviet scientists had earlier announced the discovery of element 104, but this was not accepted internationally.

Atomic Number	Elements	Symbol	Atomic Weight	Family
105	UNNIPENTIUM	Unp	262	ACTINIDE

Originally named after Otto Hahn of Germany, one of the discoverers of uranium fission. It was synthesised in 1970 by bombardment of californium with nitrogen nuclei. The name of this element was recently confirmed by the International Union of Pure and Applied Chemistry.

Onword

Once you have memorised the basic elements, and understood their properties, your brain is set for one of the most fascinating adventures imaginable!

The Solar System 19

This chapter encourages you to expand on this already expanding area of your knowledge, and to continue your journey . . .

During the last five centuries, mankind has discovered, with accelerating knowledge and fascination, that the neighbouring Planets (wanderers) of our Solar System are not simply barren rocks. Each is an astonishingly different world, with its own part to play in our search for information about our own origins.

Our Solar System's Planets include one with a surface as hot as a furnace; one with a thick blanket of clouds that veils her secrets from us and through which we are just beginning to probe; one with a surface like the deserts of Australia, and which may well sustain life; one that is bigger than all the others put together, and which has a gigantic red eye which is still not fully explained, that would swallow the Earth; one with giant rings around it and strange moons which may harbour life; one covered by vast oceans of liquid gas and a core that resembles Earth; and all the Planets are being explored as you read this book.

At this point in history, our Solar System is to us as the rest of the world was to the first European explorers: the great unknown, the arena for our next great explorations and adventures, and the environment which many of our children, grandchildren and great-grandchildren will call home.

Thus, a knowledge of our Solar System will give you your first intellectual grappling hooks into a knowledge and understanding of the universe. In so doing, it will give you a greater understanding of and perspective on your place in the scheme of all things, and will make you a part of two of man's greatest intellectual voyages: the journeys to discover the secrets of the brain and the secrets of the universe.

In this particular 'Memory Area', you are *already* an embryonic expert, for you have mastered the initial exercise and attendant explanation on pages 19–20 of chapter 3.

Brain Bites

Asteroids are huge chunks of rock, orbiting the sun between Mars and Jupiter. They are minor Planets. There may be as many as 40,000 of them.

THE SOLAR SYSTEM

	Mercury	Venus	Earth	Mars	Jupiter	Saturn	Uranus	Neptune	Pluto
Mean Distance from Sun (millions of miles)	36.0	67.1	92.9	141.5	483.4	886.7	1782.7	2794.3	3666.1
Diameter (equatorial) (miles)	3031	7521	7926	4221	88,734	74,566	31,566	30,199	1864
Mass (Earth = 1)	0.055	0.814	1.000	0.107	317.8	95.16	14.55	17.23	0.0026(?)
Density (Water = 1)	5.43	5.24	5.52	3.93	1.33	0.71	1.31	1.77	1.1
Volume (Earth = 1)	0.06	0.86	1.00	0.15	1.323	752	64	54	0.01
Revolution around Sun	88.0 days	224.7 days	365.26 days	687.0 days	11.86 yrs	29.46 yrs	84.01 yrs	164.8 yrs	247.7 yrs
Rotation Period (days)	58.65	243.0	0.9973	1.0260	0.410	0.427	0.45	0.67	6.3867
Mean Orbital Speed (miles per second)	29.8	21.7	18.6	14.9	8.0	6.0	4.2	3.3	2.9
Inclination of Orbit (to Earth's Orbital Plane)	7.0	3.4	0.0	1.8	1.3	2.5	0.8	1.8	17.2
Gravity (Earth = 1)	0.38	0.90	1.00	0.38	2.53	1.07	0.92	1.19	0.05(?)

Moons	Mercury	Venus	Earth	Mars	Jupiter	Saturn	Uranus	Neptune	Pluto
	–	–	Moon	Phobos	Io	Mimas	Ariel	Triton	Charon
				Deimos	Europa	Enceladus	Umbriel	Nereid	
					Ganymede	Tethys	Titania	Naiad	
					Callisto	Dione	Oberon	Thalassa	
					Leda	Rhea	Miranda	Despina	
					Amalthea	Titan	Cordelia	Galatea	
					Himalia	Hyperion	Ophelia	Larissa	
					Elara	Iapetus	Bianca	Proteus	
					Pasiphae	Phoebe	Cressida		
					Sinope	Janus	Desdemona		
					Lysithea	Epimetheus	Juliet		
					Carme	Helene	Portia		
					Ananke	Telesto	Rosalind		
					Thebe	Calypso	Belinda		
					Adrastea	Atlas	Puck		
					Metis	Prometheus	Caliban		
						Pandora	Sycorax		
						Pan			

Memorising Your Life:
Your Memory and Your Future

If you wish to remember the major elements of your past, present and future life, SEM³ enables you to do so with ease.

Allow one Key Memory Word for each month. In so doing, it is possible, by adding a few major items for the month on a Link System, to remember eight years within 100 Key Image Words in the Self-Enhancing Master Memory Matrix.

The memorisation of your life can be made easier and more enjoyable by using a diary/self-management system such as the Universal Personal Organiser (UPO) (*available from the Buzan Centre, see page 192*). Such a system makes use of all the Memory Principles and Techniques, organises the year, months and days in such a way as to enable you to use all your cortical and memory skills, and allows you to record, using Mind Maps and the Memory Principles, all those important aspects of your life that you consider memorable.

The dream of memorising an entire life has been one of the 'mental holy grails' of the human race. You will already have read in chapter 7 about the astonishing memory of Irenio Funes, whose feats you might have thought (before reading this book) utterly impossible. Now you know such feats are achievable, and you also know they are well worth achieving. As Jean-Jacques Rousseau, the famous French writer, philosopher and poet, wrote in 1770:

*En écrivant mes souvenirs je me rappelerai le temps passé,
qui doublera pour ainsi dire mon existence.*

**(In writing my memoirs I recall the past times which
will double, so to speak, my existence.)**

SEM^3 certainly allows you, in grasping this opportunity, to double
your existence. It will also allow you to double your appreciation
and *enjoyment* of that existence. Take the opportunity – it is now
easily within your grasp.

Conclusion – Your Future

Now that you have completed your first reading of *Master
Your Memory*, you are well on the way to providing the essential
'software' for the incredible 'hardware' of your super-
biocomputer brain.

This is a task that will give you greater mental power and
greater joy for the remainder of your life.

Since the invention of SEM^3, an increasing number of people
have become involved in networks and clubs designed to provide
companions and help on this Fantastic Voyage.

On pages 191–2 there is information on these organisations if
you wish to continue your journey . . .

Also consider entering the World Memory Championships and
exercising your memory in 'Memory Gymnasiums'. The following
websites will give you giant playgrounds in which to exercise your
Memory Muscle:

www.mind-map.com

It has been a delight sharing memory with you; I similarly look
forward to sharing *future* memories!

Recommended Reading

Atkinson, Richard C., and **Shiffrin, Richard M.** 'The Control of Short-term Memory.' *Scientific American.* August 1971.

Baddeley, Alan D. *The Psychology of Memory.* New York: Harper & Row, 1976.

Borges, Jorge L., *Fictions* (especially 'Funes, the Memorious'). London: J. Calder, 1985.

Brown, Mark. *Memory Matters.* Newton Abbot: David & Charles, 1977.

Buzan, Tony. The Mind Set: *Use Your Head, Use Your Memory, The Speed Reading Book* and *The Mind Map Book.* All London: BBC Worldwide, 2000.

Buzan, Tony. *WH Smith GCSE Revision Guides* (60).

Buzan, Tony. *Head First, The Power of Creative Intelligence, The Power of Spiritual Intelligence, The Power of Social Intelligence, The Power of Verbal Intelligence, Head Strong, How to Mind Map.* All London: Harper Collins, 2002.

Gelb, Michael J. *How to Think Like Leonardo da Vinci.* New York: Delacorte Press, 1998.

Haber, Ralph N. 'How We Remember What We See.' *Scientific American,* May 1970.

Hunt, E., and **Love, T.** 'How Good Can Memory Be?' In *Coding Processes in Human Memory,* pp. 237–60, edited by A.W. Melton and E. Martin, Washington, DC: Winston, Wiley, 1972, op.

Hunter, I.M.L., 'An Exceptional Memory', *British Journal of Psychology* **68**, 155–64, 1977.

Luria, A.R. *The Mind of a Mnemonist.* Cambridge, Mass: Harvard University Press, 1987.

North, Vanda, with **Buzan, Tony.** *Get Ahead.* UK: Buzan Centres Ltd, 1991.

Penry, J. *Looking at Faces and Remembering Them. A Guide to Facial Identification.* London: Elek Books, 1971, op.

Ruger, H.A., and **Bussenius, C. E.** *Memory.* New York: Teachers College Press, 1913 (OP).

Stratton, George M. 'The Mnemonic Feat of the "Shass Pollak".' *Physiological Review* **24**, 244–7.

Thomas, E.J. 'The Variation of Memory with Time for Information Appearing During a Lecture.' *Studies in Adult Education,* 57–62, April 1972.

Wagner, D. 'Memories of Morocco: the influence of age, schooling and environment on memory,' *Cognitive Psychology* **10**, 1–28, 1978.

Yates, F.A. *The Art of Memory.* London: Routledge & Kegan Paul, 1966; Ark, 1984.

Index

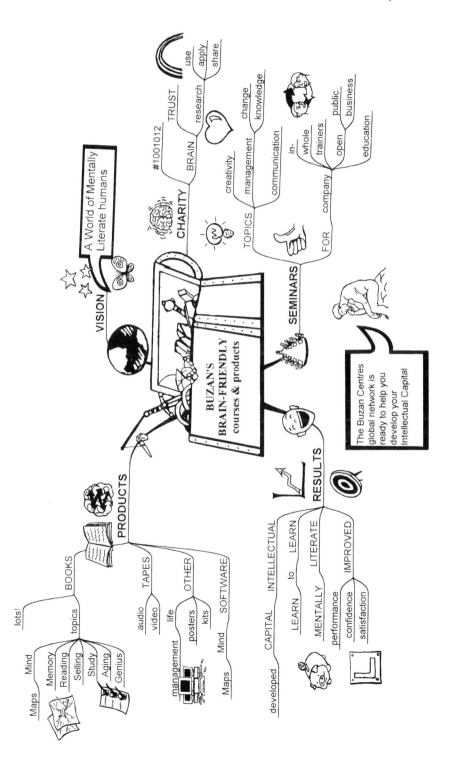

BUZAN CENTRES

Learning and Thinking
for the 21st century

We are dedicated to creating a Mentally Literate Planet –
a world where people know how to learn and think

DEVELOP YOUR INTELLECTUAL CAPITAL

with customised seminars designed to improve performance

In-Company training
Licensing for companies and independent trainers
'Open' Business Seminars
Educational Seminars

We are the ONLY organisation that can license use of the
Mind Maps® and associated trademarks

FOR FULL DETAILS OF

BUZAN LEARNING SEMINARS

and information on our range of brain-friendly products including:

- books
- software
- audio and video tapes
- support materials

SEND FOR OUR BROCHURE

Contact us at:

Buzan Centres Ltd (UK and Rest of World)
54 Parkstone Road
Poole, Dorset, BH15 2PG
Telephone: 44 (0) 1202 674676
Fax: 44 (0) 1202 674776
Email: buzan@buzancentres.com
Website: www.Mind-Map.com

BUZAN'S
BRAINFRIENDLY™

Buzan Centres Inc (Americas)
PO Box 4,Palm Beach
Florida, 33480, USA
Telephone: 001 561 881 0188
Toll free: 001 866 896 1024
Email: buzan @buzancentres.com
Website: www.Mind-Map.com

THE BRAIN TRUST CHARITY, #1001012 – invites your contribution
to assist brain research into effective processes for the enhancement of
learning, thinking and the potential of all.